English/Spanish Edition

The New Oxford Picture Dictionary

E. C. Parnwell

Translated by Sergio Gaitán

Illustrations by:
Ray Burns
Bob Giuliani
Laura Hartman
Pamela Johnson
Melodye Rosales
Raymond Skibinski
Joel Snyder

Oxford University Press

Oxford University Press

198 Madison Avenue
New York, NY 10016 USA

Great Clarendon Street
Oxford OX2 6DP England

Oxford New York

Auckland Cape Town Dar es Salaam Hong Kong Karachi
Kuala Lumpur Madrid Melbourne Mexico City Nairobi
New Delhi Shanghai Taipei Toronto

With offices in

Argentina Austria Brazil Chile Czech Republic France Greece
Guatemala Hungary Italy Japan South Korea Poland Portugal
Singapore Switzerland Thailand Turkey Ukraine Vietnam

OXFORD is a trademark of Oxford University Press

ISBN : 978 0 19 434355 8

Library of Congress Cataloging-in-Publication Data
Parnwell, E. C.
    The new Oxford picture dictionary.
    Rev. ed. of: Oxford picture dictionary of American
English. English/Spanish ed. 1978.
    Includes index.
    Summary: Teaches English as a second language to
Spanish speakers through the use of pictures dealing with
everyday topics such as the body, post office, law, travel,
and family.
    1. Picture dictionaries, English.   2. English language—
United States—Dictionaries.   3. Americanisms—
Dictionaries.   4. English Language—Textbooks for foreign
speakers—Spanish.   [1. English language—Textbooks for
foreign speakers—Spanish] I. Parnwell, E. C. Oxford
picture dictionary of American English. II. Burns,
Raymond, 1924-   , ill. III. Title. PE2835.5.P28 1989 423'.1
88-345432
ISBN : 978 0 19 434355 8

Copyright © 1989 by Oxford University Press

Developmental Editor: Margot Cramer
Associate Editor: Mary Lynne Nielsen
Art Director: Lynn Luchetti
Production Coordinator: Claire Nicholl

*The publisher would like to thank the following agents for their
cooperation:*
Carol Bancroft and Friends, representing Bob Giuliani,
Laura Hartman, and Melodye Rosales.

Publishers Graphics Inc., representing Ray Burns,
Pamela Johnson, and Joel Snyder.

Cover illustration by Laura Hartman.

Printing (last digit): 40 39 38 37 36 35 34 33

Printed in China

The New Oxford Picture Dictionary contextually illustrates over 2,400 words. The book is a unique language learning tool for students of English. It provides students with a glance at American lifestyle, as well as a compendium of useful vocabulary.

The *Dictionary* is organized thematically, beginning with topics that are most useful for the "survival" needs of students in an English-speaking country. However, pages may be used at random, depending on the students' particular needs. The book need not be taught in order.

The New Oxford Picture Dictionary contextualizes vocabulary whenever possible. Verbs have been included on separate pages, but within a topic area where they are most likely to occur. However, this does not imply that these verbs only appear within these contexts.

Articles are shown only with irregular nouns. Regional variations of the primary translation are listed following a slash (/). A complete index with pronunciation guide in English is in the Appendix.

For further ideas on using *The New Oxford Picture Dictionary*, see the *Listening and Speaking Activity Book*, the *Teacher's Guide*, and the two workbooks: *Beginner's* and *Intermediate* levels. Also available in the program are a complete set of *Cassettes*, offering a reading of all the words in the *Dictionary; Vocabulary Playing Cards*, featuring 40 words and the corresponding prictures on 80 cards, with ideas for many games; sets of *Wall Charts*, available in one complete package, or in three smaller packages; and *Overhead Transparencies*, featuring color transparencies of all the *Dictionary* pages (all of these items are available in English only). The *NOPD CD-ROM* offers the *Dictionary* in an interactive multimedia format and includes exercises and activities.

The New Oxford Picture Dictionary (El Nuevo Diccionario Ilustrado Oxford) presenta más de 2,400 palabras dentro de sus contextos. Este libro es un instrumento único en el aprendizaje de lenguas para estudiantes de inglés o de español. Además de ser un compendio de vocabulario práctico, el diccionario proporciona al alumno la oportunidad de conocer parte del estilo de vida americano.

Los temas en que está organizado el libro, comienzan con los más prácticos para alumnos principiantes en un país de habla inglesa. Sin embargo, los temas pueden utilizarse sin seguir el orden en que se presentan, y de acuerdo a las necesidades del usuario. Como libro de texto, tampoco es necesario seguir un orden.

Hasta donde ha sido posible, el *New Oxford Picture Dictionary* presenta el vocabulario dentro de un contexto. Los verbos se presentan juntos, en páginas separadas, después de ciertos temas y dentro de los contextos donde generalmente se utilizan. Estos verbos también se presentan en otros contextos.

El uso de los artículos ha sido limitado a algunos sustantivos irregulares. Cualquier variante regional de la primera traducción está en lista después de una línea diagonal (/). En el Apéndice aparece una guía para la pronunciación del inglés.

Para obtener más ideas sobre el uso del *New Oxford Picture Dictionary*, consulte la Guía del Maestro, *Teacher's Guide*, y los dos cuadernos de trabajo, (workbooks): *Beginner's and Intermediate*, Principiantes y el nivel Intermedio. Además se cuenta con un equipo de audiocintas que contienen la pronunciación de todas las palabras incluídas en el diccionario; un juego de vocabulario en tarjetas con 40 diferentes palabras con el respectivo dibujo impreso en otras 80 tarjetas separadas; y grandes láminas de las ilustraciones del libro, todo esto disponible en un sólo paquete o en tres paquetes más pequeños. Todos estos materiales se ofrecen únicamente en inglés.

iv Contents
Contenido

		Page
People and Relationships	*Gente y parentesco*	2
The Family	*La familia*	3
The Human Body	*El cuerpo humano*	4–5
Vegetables	*Legumbres/Verduras/Vegetales*	6–7
Fruits	*Frutas*	8–9
Meat, Poultry, and Seafood	*Carnes, aves, y mariscos*	10–11
Containers, Quantities, and Money	*Envases, cantidades, y dinero*	12–13
The Supermarket	*El supermercado*	14–15
Family Restaurant and Cocktail Lounge	*Restorán familiar y bar*	16
Restaurant Verbs	*Verbos relacionados con el restorán*	17
Common Prepared Foods	*Alimentos preparados comunes*	18
Outdoor Clothes	*Ropa de exteriores*	19
Everyday Clothes	*Ropa del día*	20–21
Underwear and Sleepwear	*Ropa interior y de dormir*	22
Jewelry and Cosmetics	*Joyería y cosméticos*	23
Describing Clothes	*Descripción de ropa*	24
Describing the Weather	*Descripción del clima*	25
Seasonal Verbs	*Verbos relacionados con las estaciones del año*	26
Houses	*Casas*	27
The Living Room	*La sala*	28
The Dining Room	*El comedor*	29
The Kitchen	*La cocina*	30
Kitchen Verbs	*Verbos relacionados con la cocina*	31
The Bedroom	*La recámara*	32
The Baby's Room	*El cuarto del bebé*	33
The Bathroom	*El baño*	34
The Utility Room	*El cuarto de servicios*	35
A Workshop	*Un taller de trabajo*	36–37
Housework and Repair Verbs	*Verbos relacionados con el trabajo del hogar*	38
Medical and Dental Care	*Cuidado médico y dental*	39
Ailments and Injuries	*Enfermedades y heridas*	40
Treatments and Remedies	*Tratamientos y remedios*	41
Firefighting and Rescue	*Combate del fuego y rescate*	42
Crime and Punishment	*Crimen y castigo*	43
The City	*La ciudad*	44–45
The U.S. Postal System	*El sistema postal de los Estados Unidos*	46
The Public Library	*La biblioteca pública*	47
The Armed Forces	*Las fuerzas armadas*	48
Trucks	*Camiones*	49
Cars	*Coches/Carros*	50–51
Bikes	*Bicicletas*	52
Highway Travel	*Viaje por carretera*	53
Public Transportation	*El transporte público*	54–55
Air Travel	*Viaje aéreo*	56
Aircraft	*Aviones*	57
In Port	*El puerto*	58
Pleasure Boating	*Paseo por agua*	59
Plants and Trees	*Plantas y árboles*	60–61
Simple Animals	*Animales simples*	62
Insects	*Insectos*	63
Birds	*Pájaros/Aves*	64
Fish and Reptiles	*Peces y reptiles*	65
Mammals I	*Mamíferos I*	66–67
Mammals II	*Mamíferos II*	68–69
Map of the World	*Mapa del mundo*	70–71
The United States of America	*Los Estados Unidos*	72–73
The Universe	*El universo*	74
The Space Program	*El programa espacial*	75

A Classroom	*Un salón de clase*	*Page*	76
School Verbs	*Verbos relacionados con la escuela*		77
A Science Lab	*Un laboratorio de ciencias*		78
Math	*Matemáticas*		79
Energy	*La energía*		80
Farming and Ranching	*La granja y el rancho*		81
Construction	*Construcción*		82
An Office	*Una oficina*		83
Occupations I: Main Street USA	*Ocupaciones I: La calle principal en los Estados Unidos*		84
Occupations II	*Ocupaciones II*		85
Occupations III	*Ocupaciones III*		86
Neighborhood Parks	*Parques del vecindario*		87
Outdoor Activities	*Actividades al aire libre*		88–89
At the Beach	*En la playa*		90–91
Team Sports	*Deportes en equipo*		92
Ballfields	*Campos de juego*		93
Individual Sports	*Deportes individuales*		94
Fields and Courses	*Campos y canchas de juego*		95
Sports Verbs	*Verbos relacionados con el deporte*		96–97
Musical Instruments	*Instrumentos musicales*		98
Music, Dance, and Theater	*Música, baile/danza, y teatro*		99
Electronics and Photography	*Electrónica y fotografía*		100
Handicrafts	*Trabajos manuales*		101
Prepositions of Description	*Preposiciones de descripción*		102
Prepositions of Motion	*Preposiciones de movimiento*		103
Appendix	*Apéndice*		104
Index	*Indice*		105

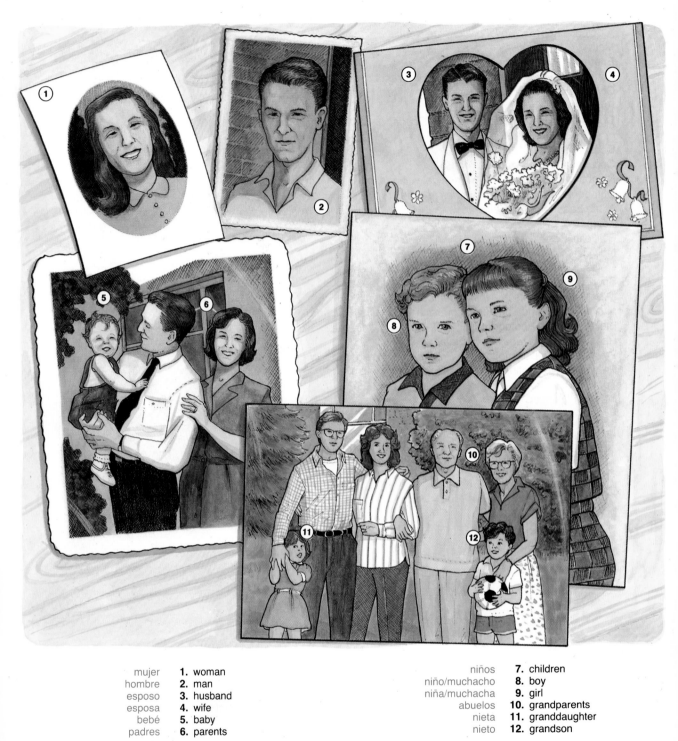

mujer	**1.** woman		niños	**7.** children
hombre	**2.** man		niño/muchacho	**8.** boy
esposo	**3.** husband		niña/muchacha	**9.** girl
esposa	**4.** wife		abuelos	**10.** grandparents
bebé	**5.** baby		nieta	**11.** granddaughter
padres	**6.** parents		nieto	**12.** grandson

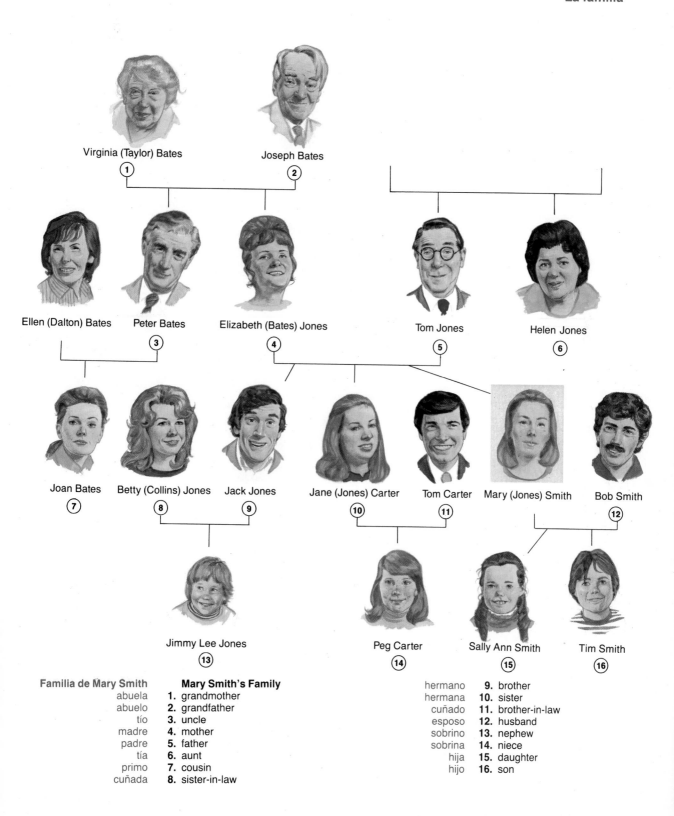

Virginia (Taylor) Bates
(1)

Joseph Bates
(2)

Ellen (Dalton) Bates

Peter Bates
(3)

Elizabeth (Bates) Jones
(4)

Tom Jones
(5)

Helen Jones
(6)

Joan Bates
(7)

Betty (Collins) Jones
(8)

Jack Jones
(9)

Jane (Jones) Carter
(10)

Tom Carter
(11)

Mary (Jones) Smith

Bob Smith
(12)

Jimmy Lee Jones
(13)

Peg Carter
(14)

Sally Ann Smith
(15)

Tim Smith
(16)

Familia de Mary Smith	Mary Smith's Family		
abuela	1. grandmother	hermano	9. brother
abuelo	2. grandfather	hermana	10. sister
tío	3. uncle	cuñado	11. brother-in-law
madre	4. mother	esposo	12. husband
padre	5. father	sobrino	13. nephew
tía	6. aunt	sobrina	14. niece
primo	7. cousin	hija	15. daughter
cuñada	8. sister-in-law	hijo	16. son

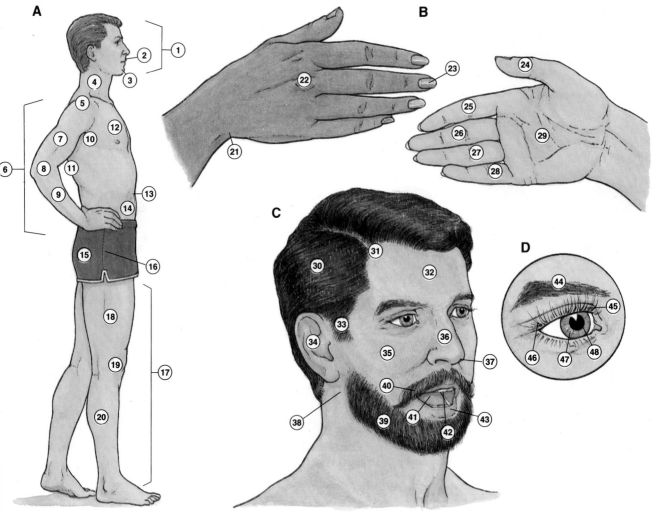

El cuerpo	A. The Body		uña	23. fingernail
cara	1. face		(dedo) pulgar	24. thumb
boca	2. mouth		índice	25. (index) finger
mentón/barbilla	3. chin		medio/dedo de enmedio	26. middle finger
cuello	4. neck		anular	27. ring finger
hombro	5. shoulder		meñique	28. little finger
brazo	6. arm		palma	29. palm
parte superior del brazo	7. upper arm			
codo	8. elbow		**La cabeza**	**C. The Head**
antebrazo	9. forearm		cabello/pelo	30. hair
axila/sobaco	10. armpit		raya/partidura	31. part
espalda	11. back		frente	32. forehead
pecho	12. chest		patilla	33. sideburn
cintura	13. waist		oreja/oído	34. ear
abdomen	14. abdomen		mejilla/cachete	35. cheek
nalgas	15. buttocks		nariz	36. nose
cadera	16. hip		orificio nasal	37. nostril
pierna	17. leg		quijada/mandíbula	38. jaw
muslo	18. thigh		barba	39. beard
rodilla	19. knee		bigote	40. mustache
pantorrilla	20. calf		lengua	41. tongue
			diente	42. tooth
La mano	**B. The Hand**		labio	43. lip
muñeca	21. wrist			
nudillo	22. knuckle			

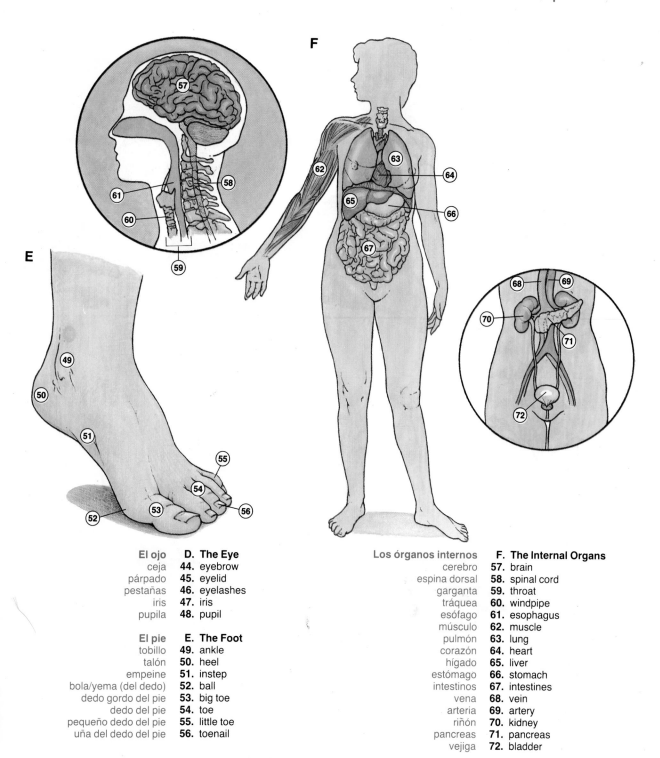

El ojo	D. The Eye
ceja	**44.** eyebrow
párpado	**45.** eyelid
pestañas	**46.** eyelashes
iris	**47.** iris
pupila	**48.** pupil

El pie	E. The Foot
tobillo	**49.** ankle
talón	**50.** heel
empeine	**51.** instep
bola/yema (del dedo)	**52.** ball
dedo gordo del pie	**53.** big toe
dedo del pie	**54.** toe
pequeño dedo del pie	**55.** little toe
uña del dedo del pie	**56.** toenail

Los órganos internos	F. The Internal Organs
cerebro	**57.** brain
espina dorsal	**58.** spinal cord
garganta	**59.** throat
tráquea	**60.** windpipe
esófago	**61.** esophagus
músculo	**62.** muscle
pulmón	**63.** lung
corazón	**64.** heart
hígado	**65.** liver
estómago	**66.** stomach
intestinos	**67.** intestines
vena	**68.** vein
arteria	**69.** artery
riñón	**70.** kidney
pancreas	**71.** pancreas
vejiga	**72.** bladder

Verduras/Legumbres/Vegetales

(cabeza de) coliflor	**1.** (head of) cauliflower
brocoli	**2.** broccoli
col/repollo	**3.** cabbage
coles pequeñas	**4.** brussels sprouts
berro	**5.** watercress
lechuga	**6.** lettuce
lechuga	**7.** escarole
espinaca	**8.** spinach
yerba(s)/hierba(s)	**9.** herb(s)
apio	**10.** celery

alcachofa	**11.** artichoke
mazorca de maíz	**12.** (ear of) corn
elote	**a.** cob
habichuela(s)/coloradas	**13.** kidney bean(s)
frijol(es) negro(s)	**14.** black bean(s)
ejote(s)/habichuelas tiernas	**15.** string bean(s)
haba(s)	**16.** lima bean(s)
chícharo(s)/petit pois	**17.** pea(s)
vaina	**a.** pod
espárragos	**18.** asparagus

(ji) tomate(s)	**19.** tomato(es)
pepino(s)	**20.** cucumber(s)
berenjena	**21.** eggplant
pimiento(s)	**22.** pepper(s)
papa(s)	**23.** potato(es)
ñame	**24.** yam
ajo	**25.** garlic
diente de ajo	**a.** clove
calabaza	**26.** pumpkin

calabacita	**27.** zucchini
calabaza pequeña	**28.** acorn squash
rábano(s)	**29.** radish(es)
hongo(s)/seta(s)	**30.** mushroom(s)
cebolla(s)	**31.** onion(s)
zanahoria(s)	**32.** carrot(s)
betabel(es)/remolacha	**33.** beet(s)
nabo	**34.** turnip

Frutas

(un racimo de) uvas	**1.** (a bunch of) grapes
manzana	**2.** apple
tallo	**a.** stem
corazón/centro	**b.** core
coco	**3.** coconut
piña	**4.** pineapple
mango	**5.** mango
papaya	**6.** papaya

Frutas cítricas	**Citrus Fruits**
toronja	**7.** grapefruit
naranja/china	**8.** orange
gajo	**a.** section
cáscara	**b.** rind
semilla/pepita	**c.** seed

limón	**9.** lemon
limón verde/lima	**10.** lime

Bayas/Frutas pequeñas	**Berries**
grosellas	**11.** gooseberries
moras/zarzamoras	**12.** blackberries
arándano agrios	**13.** cranberries
arándano azules	**14.** blueberries
fresa	**15.** strawberry
frambuesas	**16.** raspberries

nectarín	**17.** nectarine
pera	**18.** pear

cerezas	**19.** cherries		**Nueces**	**Nuts**
plátanos/guineo	**20.** (a bunch of) bananas		anacardo(s)/marañón(es)	**27.** cashew(s)
cáscara	**a.** peel		cacahuate(s)/maní	**28.** peanut(s)
			nuez (nueces) de nogal	**29.** walnut(s)
Frutas secas	**Dried Fruits**		avellana(s)	**30.** hazelnut(s)
higo	**21.** fig		almendra(s)	**31.** almond(s)
ciruela pasa	**22.** prune		castaña(s)	**32.** chestnut(s)
dátil	**23.** date			
pasa(s)	**24.** raisin(s)		aguacate/palta	**33.** avocado
			ciruela	**34.** plum
chabacano/albaricoque	**25.** apricot		melón (verde)	**35.** honeydew melon
sandía/melón	**26.** watermelon		melón	**36.** cantaloupe
			durazno/melocotón	**37.** peach
			hueso/semilla	**a.** pit
			cáscara	**b.** skin

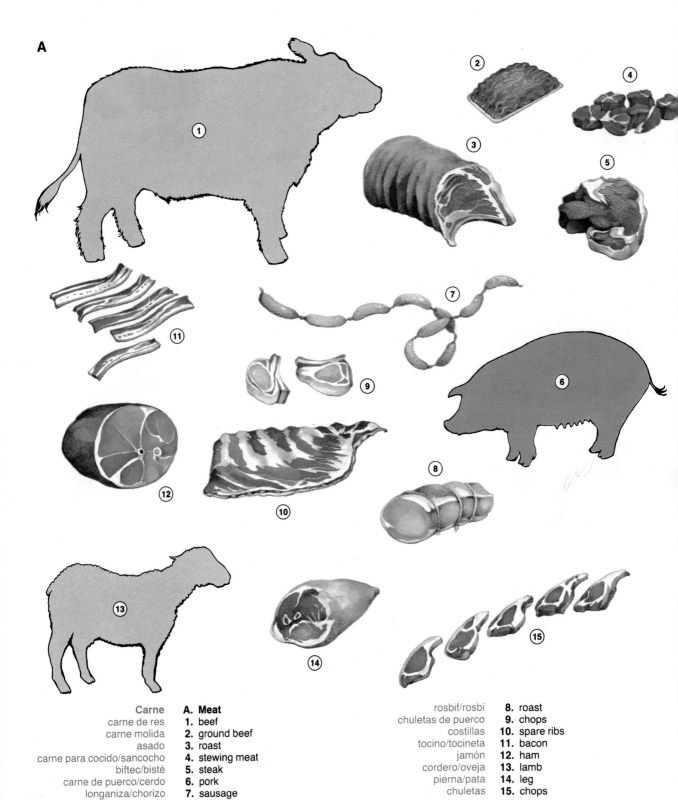

Carne	A. Meat
carne de res	1. beef
carne molida	2. ground beef
asado	3. roast
carne para cocido/sancocho	4. stewing meat
biftec/bisté	5. steak
carne de puerco/cerdo	6. pork
longaniza/chorizo	7. sausage

rosbif/rosbí	8. roast
chuletas de puerco	9. chops
costillas	10. spare ribs
tocino/tocineta	11. bacon
jamón	12. ham
cordero/oveja	13. lamb
pierna/pata	14. leg
chuletas	15. chops

B

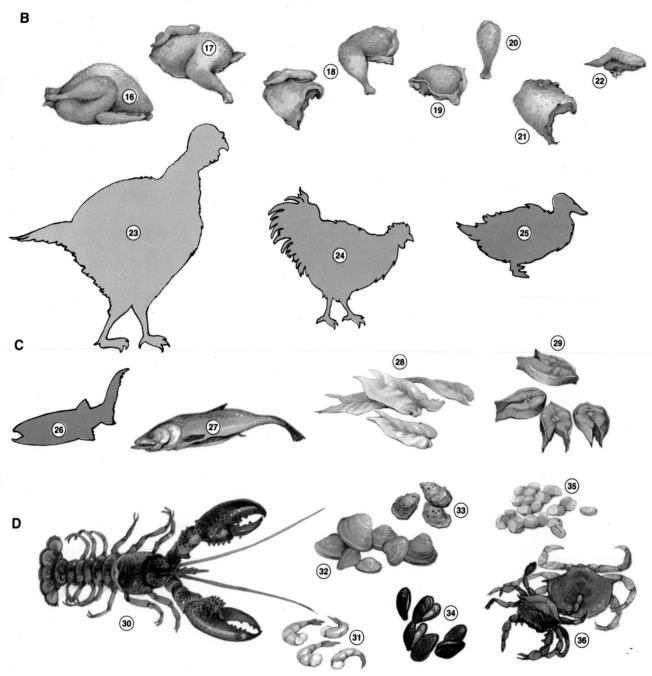

C

D

Aves de corral/pollería	**B. Poultry**		pescado entero	**27.** whole
(pollo) entero	**16.** whole (chicken)		filete	**28.** filet
medio	**17.** split		bisté	**29.** steak
un cuarto de	**18.** quarter			
muslo	**19.** thigh		**Mariscos/Moluscos**	**D. Shellfish**
pierna/pata	**20.** leg		langosta	**30.** lobster
pechuga	**21.** breast		camarón	**31.** shrimp
ala	**22.** wing		almeja(s)	**32.** clam(s)
pavo	**23.** turkey		ostión(es)/ostras	**33.** oyster(s)
pollo	**24.** chicken		mejillón(es)	**34.** mussel(s)
pato	**25.** duck		molusco(s) bivalvo(s)/escalopes	**35.** scallop(s)
Alimentos de mar/Mariscos	**C. Seafood**		jaiba(s)/juey(es)	**36.** crab(s)
pescado	**26.** fish			

cartón	**1.** carton
envase	**2.** container
botella	**3.** bottle
paquete	**4.** package
barrita	**5.** stick
batea	**6.** tub

barra de pan/hogaza de pan/ libra de pan	**7.** loaf
bolsa	**8.** bag
frasco/pote	**9.** jar
lata	**10.** can
rollo	**11.** roll

caja	**12.** box		tazón/plato hondo	**23.** bowl
paquete de seis	**13.** six-pack		lata rociadora	**24.** spray can
pompa	**14.** pump			
tubo	**15.** tube		**Dinero**	**Money**
paquete/cajetilla	**16.** pack		billete(s)	**25.** dollar bills
carterita/librito	**17.** book		monedas	**26.** coins
pastilla/barra	**18.** bar		centavo/chavito prieto	**27.** penny
taza	**19.** cup		moneda de cinco/vellón	**28.** nickel
vaso	**20.** glass		moneda de diez/sencillo	**29.** dime
rebanada	**21.** slice		moneda de veinticinco/peseta	**30.** quarter
pieza/pedazo	**22.** piece			

mostrador de fiambre y quesos	**1.** deli counter	canasta de compras	**8.** shopping basket
alimentos congelados	**2.** frozen foods	frutas y legumbres	**9.** produce
congelador	**3.** freezer	pasillo	**10.** aisle
productos lácteos	**4.** dairy products	repostería	**11.** baked goods
leche	**5.** milk	pan	**12.** bread
estante/tablilla	**6.** shelf	productos enlatados	**13.** canned goods
escala/pesa	**7.** scale	bebidas	**14.** beverages

FISH   MEAT   POULTRY

EXPRESS LANE 10 ITEMS OR LESS

artículos del hogar	**15.** household items	caja	**21.** cash register
depósito/arcón/canasta	**16.** bin	cajera/cajero	**22.** cashier
comprador/cliente	**17.** customer	banda	**23.** conveyor belt
confitería/bocadillos	**18.** snacks	abarrotes/compra	**24.** groceries
porta compras/carrito de compras	**19.** shopping cart	bolsa/funda	**25.** bag
		mostrador de chequeo	**26.** checkout counter
recibo	**20.** receipt	cheque	**27.** check

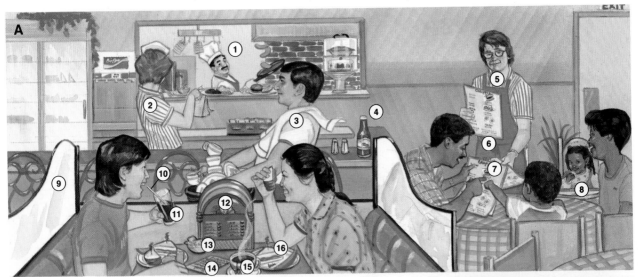

Restorán familiar	A. Family Restaurant
cocinero	1. cook
mesera	2. waitress
limpiamesas/ayudante de camarero	3. busboy
salsa de tomate/catsup	4. ketchup
mesero	5. waiter
delantal	6. apron
menú	7. menu
silla para niño/sillita	8. high chair
caseta/casilla	9. booth
popote/pitillo/sorbeto	10. straw
refresco	11. soft drink
sinfonola/vellonera	12. jukebox
(paquetito de) azúcar/(sobrecito de) azúcar	13. sugar (packet)
cuenta	14. check
té	15. tea
sandwich	16. sandwich

Bar/Cantina	B. Cocktail Lounge
sacacorcho/titabuzón	17. corkscrew
corcho	18. cork
vino	19. wine
cerveza de barril	20. tap
cantinero	21. bartender
(botella de) licor	22. liquor (bottle)
cerveza	23. beer
barra/bar	24. bar
asiento	25. bar stool
pipa	26. pipe
porta vaso	27. coaster
(carterita de) cerillos/fósforos	28. (book of) matches
cenicero	29. ashtray
encendedor	30. lighter
cigarro/cigarrillo	31. cigarette
mesera (de bebidas)	32. cocktail waitress
charola/bandeja	33. tray

Verbos relacionados con el restorán

comer	**1.** eat	colocar/poner (la mesa)	**8.** set (the table)
beber	**2.** drink	dar	**9.** give
servir	**3.** serve	tomar/agarrar	**10.** take
cocinar	**4.** cook	untar	**11.** spread
ordenar	**5.** order	sostener/aguantar	**12.** hold
recoger/limpiar	**6.** clear	encender/prender	**13.** light
pagar	**7.** pay	quemar	**14.** burn

mostaza	**1.** mustard	panecillo	**19.** roll
hot dog/perro caliente	**2.** hot dog	papa al horno	**20.** baked potato
frijoles cocidos/habichuelas cocidas	**3.** baked beans	bisté	**21.** steak
papas fritas/papitas	**4.** potato chips	galleta	**22.** cookie
panqueques/pancakes	**5.** pancakes	sundae	**23.** sundae
almíbar	**6.** syrup	taco	**24.** taco
panecillo	**7.** bun	rollo relleno de carne con verduras	**25.** egg roll
pepinillo	**8.** pickle	pastelillo de fresa	**26.** strawberry shortcake
hamburguesa	**9.** hamburger	bisquet/panecillo	**27.** biscuit
espagueti	**10.** spaghetti	papas fritas	**28.** french fries
albóndigas	**11.** meatballs	pollo frito	**29.** fried chicken
aderezo	**12.** salad dressing	pizza	**30.** pizza
ensalada	**13.** tossed salad	jalea	**31.** jelly
asado/sancocho	**14.** beef stew	huevo (estrellado)	**32.** (sunnyside-up) egg
chuletas de puerco	**15.** pork chops	tocino/tocineta	**33.** bacon
verduras mixtas/vegetales mixtos	**16.** mixed vegetables	pan tostado/tostada	**34.** toast
puré de papas/papas majadas	**17.** mashed potatoes	café	**35.** coffee
mantequilla	**18.** butter	barquillo de nieve/helado/barquilla	**36.** ice cream cone

guantes	**1.**	gloves
gorra	**2.**	cap
camisa de franela	**3.**	flannel shirt
mochila	**4.**	backpack
rompeviento	**5.**	windbreaker
pantalón de mezclilla/mahón	**6.**	(blue) jeans
suéter (cerrado)	**7.**	(crewneck) sweater
abrigo de invierno/chamarra de invierno	**8.**	parka
botas de excursionismo	**9.**	hiking boots
orejeras	**10.**	earmuffs
guante entero/mitón	**11.**	mittens
chaleco de plumas de ganso	**12.**	down vest
suéter (cuello de tortuga)	**13.**	(turtleneck) sweater
medias de invierno	**14.**	tights
patines de hielo	**15.**	ice skates
gorro de esquiar	**16.**	ski cap
chaqueta/chamarra	**17.**	jacket
sombrero	**18.**	hat
bufanda	**19.**	scarf
sobreabrigo	**20.**	overcoat
botas	**21.**	boots
boina	**22.**	beret
suéter (cuello V)	**23.**	(V-neck) sweater
abrigo/sobretodo	**24.**	coat
botas de lluvia	**25.**	rain boots

solapa	**1.** lapel	pantaloncillo/shorts	**14.** shorts
saco ''sport''	**2.** blazer	manga larga	**15.** long sleeve
botón	**3.** button	cinturón/correa	**16.** belt
pantalón	**4.** slacks	hebilla	**17.** buckle
tacón	**5.** heel	bolsa de compras	**18.** shopping bag
suela	**6.** sole	sandalia	**19.** sandal
agujeta/cordón/gavetes	**7.** shoelace	cuello	**20.** collar
sudadera	**8.** sweatshirt	manga corta	**21.** short sleeve
cartera/billetera	**9.** wallet	vestido	**22.** dress
pantalón de sudadera/pants	**10.** sweatpants	bolso/cartera	**23.** purse
tenis	**11.** sneakers	paraguas/sombrilla	**24.** umbrella
banda/cinta	**12.** sweatband	zapatos de tacón (alto)	**25.** (high) heels
camiseta sin mangas	**13.** tank top		

suéter abierto	26. cardigan	impermeable/capa de agua	38. raincoat
pantalón (de pana)	27. (corduroy) pants	chaleco	39. vest
sombrero duro/casco	28. hard hat	traje de tres piezas	40. three-piece suit
camiseta manga corta	29. T-shirt	bolsa/bolsillo	41. pocket
overol/mameluco	30. overalls	mocasín	42. loafer
lonchera	31. lunch box	cachucha/gorra	43. cap
botas	32. (construction) boots	lentes/anteojos/gafas	44. glasses
saco de vestir	33. jacket	uniforme	45. uniform
blusa	34. blouse	camisa	46. shirt
bolso	35. (shoulder) bag	corbata	47. tie
falda	36. skirt	periódico	48. newspaper
portafolio/maletín	37. briefcase	zapato	49. shoe

camiseta	**1.** undershirt		pantaleta	**12.** briefs
calzoncillo boxer	**2.** boxer shorts		sostén/porta bustos	**13.** bra(ssiere)
calzón/calzoncillo	**3.** underpants		liguero	**14.** garter belt
suspensorio	**4.** athletic supporter		faja	**15.** girdle
pantimedia	**5.** pantyhose		calcetines largos	**16.** knee socks
medias	**6.** stockings		calcetines/medias	**17.** socks
calzón largo	**7.** long johns		pantuflas/chancletas	**18.** slippers
medio fondo/enagua	**8.** half slip		pijamas	**19.** pajamas
camisola/bustillo	**9.** camisole		bata (de baño)	**20.** bathrobe
fondo entero/refajo	**10.** full slip		camisón/bata de noche	**21.** nightgown
pantaleta (bikini)	**11.** (bikini) panties			

Joyería/Prendas

aretes/pantallas
anillo(s)/sortija(s)
anillo de compromiso/sortija de compromiso
anillo de boda/ sortija de boda
cadena
collar
(collar de) cuentas
prendedor
pulsera/brazalete
reloj de pulsera
extensible/correa de reloj
mancuernas/yuntas
prendedor/alfiler de corbata
broche de corbata
arete de presión/pantalla de pinchar
arete de broche/pantalla de gancho
broche

A. Jewelry
1. earrings
2. ring(s)
3. engagement ring

4. wedding ring
5. chain
6. necklace
7. (strand of) beads
8. pin
9. bracelet
10. watch
11. watchband
12. cuff links
13. tie pin
14. tie clip
15. clip-on earring

16. pierced earring

17. clasp

frente/gancho
trasero/atrás

Artículos de tocador y maquillaje

rastrillo
loción para después de afeitar
crema de afeitar
navajas para afeitar
lima
esmalte para uñas
lápiz para cejas
perfume
máscara
lápiz labial
sombra para ojos
cortauñas
rubor/colorete
delineador

18. post
19. back

B. Toiletries and Makeup

20. razor
21. after-shave lotion
22. shaving cream
23. razor blades
24. emery board
25. nail polish
26. eyebrow pencil
27. perfume
28. mascara
29. lipstick
30. eye shadow
31. nail clippers
32. blush
33. eyeliner

corta	**1.** short	bajo	**12.** low
larga	**2.** long	nueva	**13.** new
apretado	**3.** tight	vieja	**14.** old
flojo/suelto/holgado	**4.** loose	abierto	**15.** open
sucio	**5.** dirty	cerrado	**16.** closed
limpio	**6.** clean	rayado/de líneas (rayitas)	**17.** striped
chico/pequeño	**7.** small	a cuadros/de cuadritos	**18.** checked
grande	**8.** big	punteado/de bolitas	**19.** polka dot
claro	**9.** light	sólido/entero (color)	**20.** solid
obscuro	**10.** dark	estampado	**21.** print
alto	**11.** high	diseño a cuadros/madras	**22.** plaid

lluvioso	**1.** rainy	fresco	**9.** cool
nublado	**2.** cloudy	frío	**10.** cold
con nieve/nevado	**3.** snowy	helando/helado	**11.** freezing
soleado	**4.** sunny	con neblina	**12.** foggy
termómetro	**5.** thermometer	con viento	**13.** windy
temperatura	**6.** temperature	seco	**14.** dry
caliente	**7.** hot	mojado	**15.** wet
caluroso	**8.** warm	helado/congelado (y resbaloso)	**16.** icy

Verbos relacionados con las estaciones del año

Primavera	Spring	Verano	Summer	Otoño	Fall	Invierno	Winter
pintar	**1.** paint	regar	**5.** water	llenar	**9.** fill	traspalar/palear	**13.** shovel
limpiar	**2.** clean	cortar el césped/cortar la grama	**6.** mow	rastrillar	**10.** rake	enarenar	**14.** sand
excavar	**3.** dig	recoger	**7.** pick	cortar	**11.** chop	raspar	**15.** scrape
plantar	**4.** plant	recortar/podar	**8.** trim	empujar	**12.** push	cargar	**16.** carry

A

B

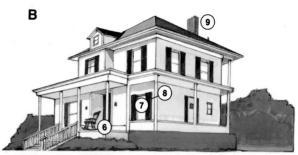

C

Casa de rancho	**A. Ranch House**
entrada de carro	**1.** driveway
garaje/marquesina	**2.** garage
antena de televisión	**3.** TV antenna
techo	**4.** roof
asoleadera	**5.** deck
Casa estilo colonial	**B. Colonial-style House**
porche/balcón	**6.** porch
ventana	**7.** window
contraventana	**8.** shutter
chimenea	**9.** chimney
El patio interior	**C. The Backyard**
gotera/desagüe	**10.** gutter
hamaca	**11.** hammock
cortadora de césped (grama)	**12.** lawn mower
rociador/regadera	**13.** sprinkler
manguera	**14.** garden hose
césped/pasto/grama	**15.** grass

regadera de mano	**16.** watering can
patio	**17.** patio
desagüe de lluvia	**18.** drainpipe
mosquitero	**19.** screen
guante	**20.** mitt
espátula	**21.** spatula
parrilla	**22.** grill
carbón	**23.** charcoal briquettes
soleadero	**24.** lounge chair
sierra eléctrica	**25.** power saw
guantes de trabajo	**26.** work gloves
cuchara (de albañil)/pala de jardín	**27.** trowel
tejadillo de herramientas	**28.** toolshed
tijeras de césped	**29.** hedge clippers
rastrillo	**30.** rake
pala	**31.** shovel
carretilla	**32.** wheelbarrow

ventilador de techo	**1.**	ceiling fan
techo	**2.**	ceiling
pared	**3.**	wall
marco/cuadro	**4.**	frame
pintura	**5.**	painting
jarrón	**6.**	vase
repisa	**7.**	mantel
chimenea	**8.**	fireplace
fuego	**9.**	fire
leña	**10.**	log
pasamano	**11.**	banister
escalera	**12.**	staircase
escalón	**13.**	step
escritorio	**14.**	desk
alfombrado (de pared a pared)	**15.**	wall-to-wall carpeting

reclinador	**16.**	recliner
control remoto	**17.**	remote control
televisor	**18.**	television
mueble de pared	**19.**	wall unit
estéreo	**20.**	stereo system
bocina	**21.**	speaker
librero	**22.**	bookcase
cortinas	**23.**	drapes
cojín	**24.**	cushion
sofá	**25.**	sofa
mesita central	**26.**	coffee table
pantalla de lámpara	**27.**	lampshade
lámpara	**28.**	lamp
mesita	**29.**	end table

vajilla/loza	**1.** china	mantel	**16.** tablecloth
armario/alacena de loza/chinero	**2.** china closet	silla	**17.** chair
candil	**3.** chandelier	cafetera	**18.** coffeepot
jarra	**4.** pitcher	tetera	**19.** teapot
copa de vino	**5.** wine glass	taza	**20.** cup
vaso	**6.** water glass	platito/platillo	**21.** saucer
mesa	**7.** table	juego de cubiertos	**22.** silverware
cuchara	**8.** spoon	azucarera	**23.** sugar bowl
pimentero	**9.** pepper shaker	cremera	**24.** creamer
salero	**10.** salt shaker	ensaladera	**25.** salad bowl
platito para mantequilla y pan	**11.** bread and butter plate	flama/llama	**26.** flame
tenedor	**12.** fork	vela	**27.** candle
plato	**13.** plate	candelero	**28.** candlestick
servilleta	**14.** napkin	aparador/mostrador	**29.** buffet
cuchillo	**15.** knife		

lavaplatos/máquina de lavar platos	**1.** dishwasher	secador/paño de platos	**18.** dish towel
escurridor	**2.** dish drainer	refrigerador/nevera	**19.** refrigerator
vaporera	**3.** steamer	congelador	**20.** freezer
abrelatas	**4.** can opener	charola para cubitos de hielo/ cubeta de hielo	**21.** ice tray
sartén	**5.** frying pan	gabinete	**22.** cabinet
destapador	**6.** bottle opener	horno microondas	**23.** microwave oven
coladera/colador	**7.** colander	molde	**24.** mixing bowl
cacerola/olla	**8.** saucepan	rodillo/rolo	**25.** rolling pin
tapa	**9.** lid	picador/tabla para cortar	**26.** cutting board
jabón líquido para trastes/jabón de fregar	**10.** dishwashing liquid	mostrador	**27.** counter
cojincillo de restregar/brillo	**11.** scouring pad	tetera	**28.** teakettle
licuadora	**12.** blender	quemador/hornilla	**29.** burner
olla/caldero	**13.** pot	estufa	**30.** stove
cacerola	**14.** casserole dish	cafetera	**31.** coffeemaker
latería	**15.** canister	horno	**32.** oven
tostador	**16.** toaster	asador	**33.** broiler
cazuela/bandeja de asar	**17.** roasting pan	sostén de ollas/agarradera	**34.** pot holder

menear/revolver	**1.** stir	cortar	**9.** cut
gratinar/moler	**2.** grate	rebanar	**10.** slice
abrir	**3.** open	picar	**11.** chop
echar/servir	**4.** pour	cocinar a vapor	**12.** steam
pelar/mondar	**5.** peel	asar	**13.** broil
cortar/tajar	**6.** carve	hornear	**14.** bake
romper	**7.** break	freir	**15.** fry
batir	**8.** beat	hervir	**16.** boil

gancho	**1.** hook	colchón	**17.** mattress
gancho para ropa	**2.** hanger	colchón de muelles	**18.** box spring
closet	**3.** closet	sábana	**19.** (flat) sheet
joyero	**4.** jewelry box	cobija	**20.** blanket
espejo	**5.** mirror	cama	**21.** bed
peine/peinilla	**6.** comb	cobertor acolchado	**22.** comforter
cepillo de pelo	**7.** hairbrush	colcha/sobrecama	**23.** bedspread
despertador	**8.** alarm clock	pie de la cama	**24.** footboard
buró/gavetero/ropero	**9.** bureau	interruptor de luz/apagador	**25.** light switch
cortina	**10.** curtain	teléfono	**26.** phone
aire acondicionado	**11.** air conditioner	cordón	**a.** cord
persianas	**12.** blinds	conexión/enchufe	**b.** jack
pañuelos faciales	**13.** tissues	nochero/mesita de noche	**27.** night table
cabecera	**14.** headboard	alfombra/tapete	**28.** rug
funda	**15.** pillowcase	piso	**29.** floor
almohada	**16.** pillow	cómoda/gavetero	**30.** chest of drawers

cortinilla	**1.**	shade
móvil	**2.**	mobile
oso de peluche	**3.**	teddy bear
cuna	**4.**	crib
colchón protector/orillero	**5.**	bumper
loción para bebé	**6.**	baby lotion
talco para bebé	**7.**	baby powder
toallitas para bebé	**8.**	baby wipes
mesita (portátil)	**9.**	changing table
cotonete/algodoncito/palitos de algodón	**10.**	cotton swab
seguro/imperdibles	**11.**	safety pin
pañal desechable	**12.**	disposable diaper
pañal	**13.**	cloth diaper
carrito de bebé	**14.**	stroller
detector de humo	**15.**	smoke detector
(silla) mecedora	**16.**	rocking chair

biberón	**17.**	bottle
tetilla/pezón/mamadera	**18.**	nipple
trajecito	**19.**	stretchie
babero	**20.**	bib
sonaja/maraquita	**21.**	rattle
chupón	**22.**	pacifier
andadera/andador	**23.**	walker
columpio	**24.**	swing
casa de muñecas	**25.**	doll house
cuna mecedora	**26.**	cradle
animal de peluche	**27.**	stuffed animal
muñeca	**28.**	doll
juguetero/baúl de juguetes	**29.**	toy chest
corral de juego	**30.**	playpen
rompecabezas	**31.**	puzzle
bloques	**32.**	block
basinica/escupidera	**33.**	potty

cortinero/palo de cortina	**1.** curtain rod	llave del agua caliente	**17.** hot water faucet
aros para cortina	**2.** curtain rings	llave del agua fría	**18.** cold water faucet
gorro de baño	**3.** shower cap	lavabo/lavamanos	**19.** sink
regadera/ducha	**4.** shower head	cepillo para uñas	**20.** nailbrush
cortina de baño	**5.** shower curtain	cepillo de dientes	**21.** toothbrush
jabonera	**6.** soap dish	toallita	**22.** washcloth
esponja	**7.** sponge	toalla de manos	**23.** hand towel
shampú/champú	**8.** shampoo	toalla de baño	**24.** bath towel
drenaje/desagüe	**9.** drain	toallero	**25.** towel rack
tapón	**10.** stopper	secador	**26.** hair dryer
tina/bañera	**11.** bathtub	azulejo/loseta	**27.** tile
tapete de baño/alfombra de baño	**12.** bath mat	canasto	**28.** hamper
basurero/zafacón	**13.** wastepaper basket	excusado/inodoro	**29.** toilet
botiquín	**14.** medicine chest	papel de baño/papel higiénico	**30.** toilet paper
jabón	**15.** soap	cepillo de baño	**31.** toilet brush
pasta de dientes	**16.** toothpaste	báscula/pesa	**32.** scale

escalera	**1.** stepladder	accesorios	**17.** attachments
plumero/sacudidor	**2.** feather duster	tubo	**18.** pipe
lámpara (de mano)	**3.** flashlight	tendedero	**19.** clothesline
trapos	**4.** rags	pinzas/pinches de ropa	**20.** clothespins
caja de fusibles/corta circuitos	**5.** circuit breaker	almidón en lata rociadora	**21.** spray starch
limpiador (de esponja)	**6.** (sponge) mop	foco/bombilla	**22.** lightbulb
escoba	**7.** broom	papel absorbente	**23.** paper towels
recogedor	**8.** dustpan	secadora	**24.** dryer
limpiador en polvo	**9.** cleanser	detergente	**25.** laundry detergent
líquido limpia ventanas	**10.** window cleaner	blanqueador	**26.** bleach
repuesto	**11.** (mop) refill	suavizante	**27.** fabric softener
plancha	**12.** iron	lavandería	**28.** laundry
mesa de planchar	**13.** ironing board	canasto de lavandería	**29.** laundry basket
bomba/destapa caños	**14.** plunger	lavadora	**30.** washing machine
cubeta/cubo	**15.** bucket	basurero/zafacón	**31.** garbage can
aspiradora	**16.** vacuum cleaner	ratonera	**32.** mousetrap

regla de carpintero	**1.** carpenter's rule	martillo	**13.** hammer
tornillo de banco	**2.** C-clamp	espátula/alijadora	**14.** scraper
sierra	**3.** jigsaw	tablero para colgar	**15.** pegboard
madera	**4.** wood	herramientas	
extensión	**5.** extension cord	gancho	**16.** hook
contacto/enchufe	**6.** outlet	hacha	**17.** hatchet
clavija de tierra	**7.** grounding plug	serrucho	**18.** hacksaw
serrote/serrucho	**8.** saw	pinzas/alicate	**19.** pliers
taladro de mano	**9.** brace	sierra circular	**20.** circular saw
llave de tuercas/llave de perro	**10.** wrench	cinta de medir	**21.** tape measure
mazo	**11.** mallet	mesa de trabajo	**22.** workbench
llave inglesa	**12.** monkey wrench	caja de herramientas	**23.** toolbox

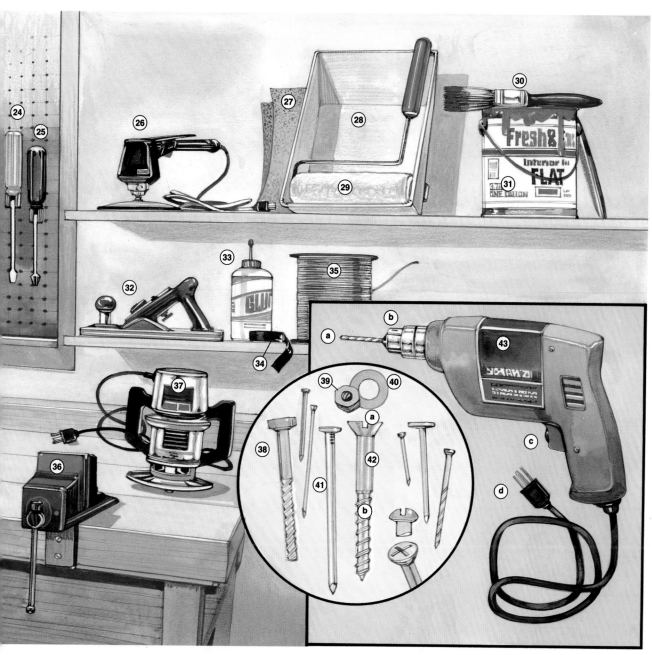

destornillador/desarmador	**24.** screwdriver
desarmador Phillips	**25.** Phillips screwdriver
pulidora	**26.** power sander
lija	**27.** sandpaper
cacerola/bandeja	**28.** pan
rodillo	**29.** roller
brocha	**30.** paintbrush
pintura	**31.** paint
cepillo de madera	**32.** wood plane
pegamento	**33.** glue
cinta de aislar	**34.** electrical tape
cable eléctrico	**35.** wire
tornillo de banco	**36.** vise

canalizador/ranurador	**37.** router
perno/tornillo grande	**38.** bolt
tuerca	**39.** nut
rondalla/arandela	**40.** washer
clavo	**41.** nail
tornillo	**42.** screw
cabeza	**a.** head
rosca	**b.** thread
taladro eléctrico	**43.** electric drill
taladro	**a.** bit
astil	**b.** shank
interruptor	**c.** switch
clavija	**d.** plug

doblar	**1.** fold	secar	**9.** dry
tallar/restregar	**2.** scrub	reparar	**10.** repair
lustrar/pulir	**3.** polish	planchar	**11.** iron
apretar	**4.** tighten	aceitar	**12.** oil
secar/limpiar	**5.** wipe	cambiar (las sábanas)	**13.** change (the sheets)
colgar	**6.** hang	aspirar	**14.** vacuum
barrer	**7.** sweep	sacudir	**15.** dust
hacer/tender (la cama)	**8.** make (the bed)	lavar	**16.** wash

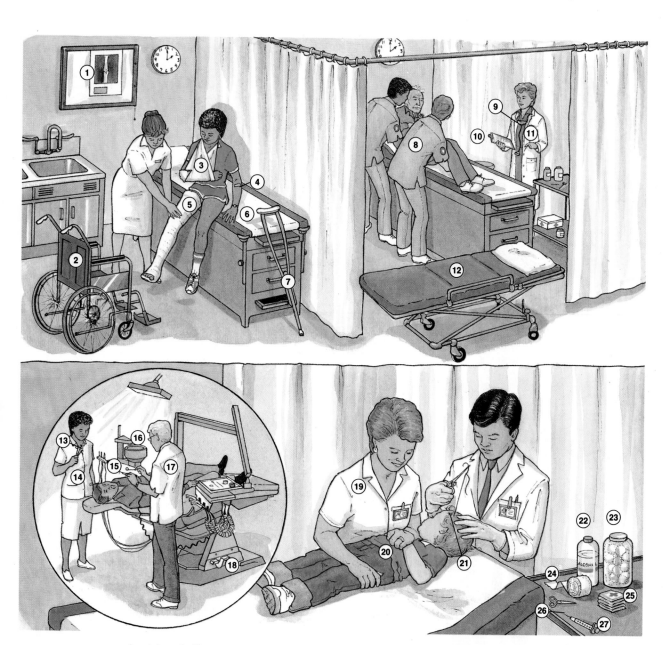

rayos x (equis)	**1.** X ray		taladro	**15.** drill
silla de ruedas	**2.** wheelchair		escupidero	**16.** basin
soporte	**3.** sling		dentista	**17.** dentist
curita	**4.** Band-Aid		pedal	**18.** pedal
enyesado	**5.** cast		enfermera	**19.** nurse
mesa de reconocimiento	**6.** examining table		paciente	**20.** patient
muleta	**7.** crutch		puntadas/puntos	**21.** stitches
ayudante	**8.** attendant		alcohol	**22.** alcohol
estetoscopio	**9.** stethoscope		algodón	**23.** cotton balls
cuadro médico	**10.** chart		vendas (de gaza)	**24.** (gauze) bandage
doctor	**11.** doctor		gaza	**25.** gauze pads
camilla	**12.** stretcher		aguja	**26.** needle
instrumentos	**13.** instruments		jeringa	**27.** syringe
higienista bucal	**14.** oral hygienist			

sarpullido	**1.**	rash
fiebre	**2.**	fever
piquete de insecto/picada	**3.**	insect bite
resfríos/escalofríos	**4.**	chills
ojo morado	**5.**	black eye
dolor de cabeza	**6.**	headache
dolor de estómago	**7.**	stomachache
dolor de espalda	**8.**	backache
dolor de muela	**9.**	toothache
alta presión sanguínea/presión alta	**10.**	high blood pressure
resfriado/resfrío	**11.**	cold
dolor de garganta	**12.**	sore throat
depresor de lengua/paleta		**a.** tongue depressor
torcedura	**13.**	sprain
venda elástica		**a.** stretch bandage
infección	**14.**	infection
fractura	**15.**	broken bone
cortada	**16.**	cut
golpe	**17.**	bruise
quemadura	**18.**	burn

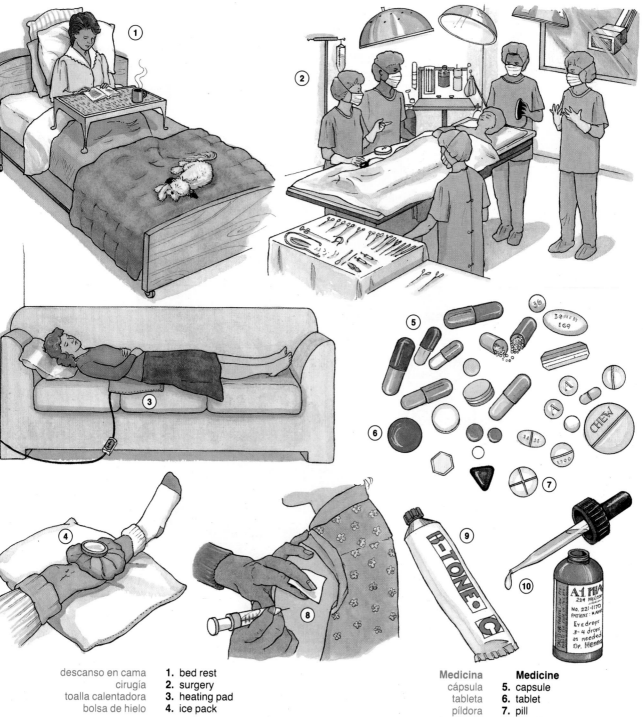

descanso en cama	**1.** bed rest
cirugía	**2.** surgery
toalla calentadora	**3.** heating pad
bolsa de hielo	**4.** ice pack

Medicina	**Medicine**
cápsula	**5.** capsule
tableta	**6.** tablet
píldora	**7.** pill
inyección	**8.** injection
ungüento	**9.** ointment
gotas para los ojos	**10.** eye drops

escalera	**1.** ladder	bomba de agua para incendios	**9.** fire hydrant
carro tanque de bomberos/	**2.** fire engine	bombero	**10.** fire fighter
carro bombas		extinguidor	**11.** fire extinguisher
carro de bomberos	**3.** fire truck	casco	**12.** helmet
escape de incendio	**4.** fire escape	abrigo	**13.** coat
fuego/incendio	**5.** fire	hacha	**14.** ax
ambulancia	**6.** ambulance	humo	**15.** smoke
enfermero/paramédico	**7.** paramedic	agua	**16.** water
manguera	**8.** hose	lanza agua	**17.** nozzle

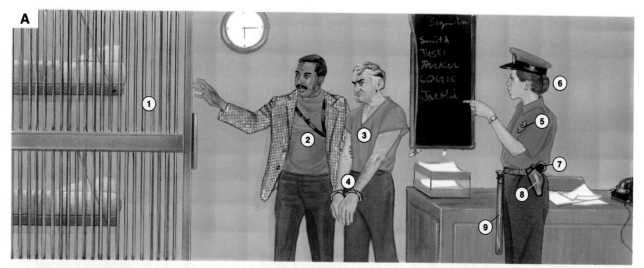

Estación de policía	**A. Police Station**		martillo	**12.** gavel
cárcel	**1.** jail		testigo	**13.** witness
detective	**2.** detective		anotador	**14.** court reporter
sospechoso	**3.** suspect		transcripción	**15.** transcript
esposas	**4.** handcuffs		tribunal/banco	**16.** bench
escudo/insignia/chapa	**5.** badge		fiscal acusador	**17.** prosecuting attorney
(oficial de) policía	**6.** police officer		tribuna del testigo/silla del	**18.** witness stand
arma/pistola/revólver	**7.** gun		testigo	
funda/baqueta	**8.** holster		oficial de la corte	**19.** court officer
macana	**9.** nightstick		tribunal del jurado	**20.** jury box
			jurado	**21.** jury
Corte/Sala de Juicio	**B. Court**		abogado defensor	**22.** defense attorney
juez	**10.** judge		demandado/acusado	**23.** defendant
bata	**11.** robes		huellas digitales	**24.** fingerprints

edificio de oficinas	**1.** office building
recibidor	**2.** lobby
esquina	**3.** corner
vía peatonal	**4.** crosswalk
tienda de departamentos	**5.** department store
panadería/pastelería	**6.** bakery
teléfono público	**7.** public telephone
letrero	**8.** street sign
oficina de correo	**9.** post office

policía de tránsito	**10.** traffic cop
cruce	**11.** intersection
peatón	**12.** pedestrian
parada de autobús	**13.** bus stop
banca	**14.** bench
basurero/zafacón	**15.** trash basket
estación del metro/estación del subterráneo	**16.** subway station

ck Out Receipt

Codman Square Branch Library
-436-8214
):://www.bpl.org/branches/codman.htm

Jay, October 13, 2023 9:58:07 AM

1: 39999052039953
le: Word by word picture dictionary
erial: Book
: 11/3/2023

1: 39999069496196
le: The new Oxford picture diction
erial: Book
: 11/3/2023

al items: 2

ık You!

elevador/ascensor	**17.** elevator	acera/banqueta	**25.** sidewalk
librería	**18.** bookstore	reborde/cuneta	**26.** curb
estacionamiento	**19.** parking garage	carro para bebé	**27.** baby carriage
parquímetro	**20.** parking meter	mercado de frutas y legumbres	**28.** fruit and vegetable market
semáforo	**21.** traffic light	poste de luz	**29.** streetlight
farmacia	**22.** drugstore	puesto de periódicos y revistas	**30.** newsstand
apartamentos	**23.** apartment house	calle	**31.** street
número del edificio	**24.** building number	alcantarilla	**32.** manhole

Entrega de correo	A. **Delivering Mail**	Oficina de correos	B. **The Post Office**
buzón	1. mailbox	ranura	13. mail slot
correo	2. mail	empleado postal	14. postal worker
cartero	3. letter carrier	ventanilla	15. window
bolsa de correo	4. mailbag		
camión de correo	5. mail truck	**Tipos de correo**	C. **Types of Mail**
buzón de los Estados Unidos	6. U.S. mailbox	sobre (aéreo)	16. (airmail) envelope
carta	7. letter	tarjeta postal	17. postcard
remitente	8. return address	orden monetaria/giro postal	18. money order
sello de correo	9. postmark	paquete	19. package
estampilla/timbre (de correo)	10. stamp	cordón/cuerda	20. string
dirección	11. address	etiqueta	21. label
código postal/área postal	12. zip code	cinta	22. tape
		(paquete) correo express	23. Express Mail (package)

empleado de biblioteca	**1.** library clerk	sección de revistas/	**15.** periodicals section
mostrador de chequeo	**2.** checkout desk	publicaciones periódicas	
tarjeta de biblioteca	**3.** library card	revista	**16.** magazine
catálogo/tarjetero	**4.** card catalog	estante	**17.** rack
cajón/gaveta	**5.** drawer	fotocopiadora/sacacopias	**18.** photocopy machine
tarjeta informativa	**6.** call card	globo/esfera	**19.** globe
número de clasificación	**7.** call number	atlas	**20.** atlas
autor	**8.** author	sección de referencia	**21.** reference section
título	**9.** title	información	**22.** information desk
tema/materia	**10.** subject	bibliotecaria	**23.** (reference) librarian
fila	**11.** row	diccionario	**24.** dictionary
ficha de reclamo	**12.** call slip	enciclopedia	**25.** encyclopedia
microfilm	**13.** microfilm	repisa/tablilla	**26.** shelf
amplificador de microfilm	**14.** microfilm reader		

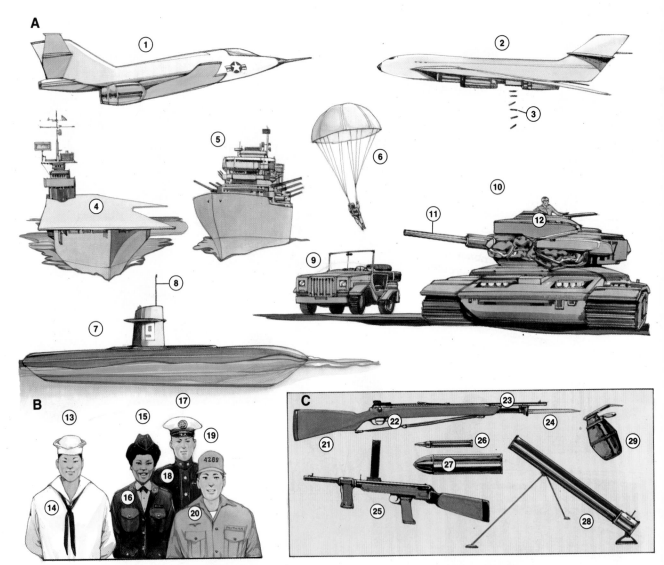

Vehículos y equipo

avión de caza
bombardero
bomba
portaviones
barco de guerra
paracaídas
submarino
periscopio
jeep
tanque
cañón
torre blindada de armas

A. Vehicles and Equipment

1. fighter plane
2. bomber
3. bomb
4. aircraft carrier
5. battleship
6. parachute
7. submarine
8. periscope
9. jeep
10. tank
11. cannon
12. gun turret

Personal

Naval/Marina
marinero

B. Personnel

13. Navy
14. sailor

Armada/Ejército
soldado
Marina
marino
Fuerza Aérea
aviador

15. Army
16. soldier
17. Marines
18. marine
19. Air Force
20. airman

Armas y munición

rifle
gatillo
cañón
bayoneta
ametralladora
bala
casquillo
mortero
granada (de mano)

C. Weapons and Ammunition

21. rifle
22. trigger
23. barrel
24. bayonet
25. machine gun
26. bullet
27. shell
28. mortar
29. hand grenade

barredora/limpia calles	**1.** street cleaner	persona de entrega	**10.** delivery person
grúa	**2.** tow truck	carro de mudanza	**11.** moving van
carro tanque	**3.** fuel truck	mudador	**12.** mover
camioneta	**4.** pickup truck	mezcladora de cemento/	**13.** cement truck
pala de nieve	**5.** snow plow	revolvedora de cemento	
camión de la basura	**6.** garbage truck	camión de volteo	**14.** dump truck
empleado de limpieza	**7.** sanitation worker	trailer	**15.** tractor trailer
camioneta de lonchar/cantina	**8.** lunch truck	chofer/camionero	**16.** truck driver
rodante		transportador/porta autos	**17.** transporter
camión	**9.** panel truck	acoplado	**18.** flatbed

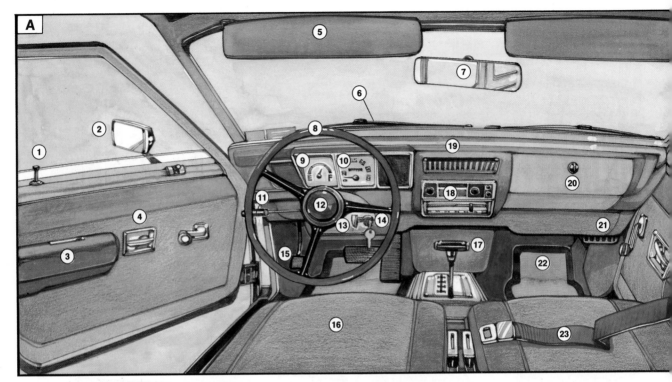

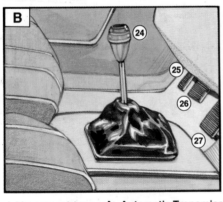

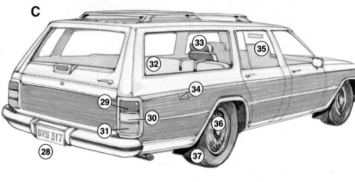

Transmisión automática	A. Automatic Transmission
seguro	1. door lock
espejo lateral	2. side mirror
descansa brazo	3. armrest
manija	4. door handle
visera	5. visor
limpiador/limpia parabrisas	6. windshield wiper
espejo retrovisor	7. rearview mirror
volante/guía	8. steering wheel
medidor de (la) gasolina	9. gas gauge
velocímetro	10. speedometer
palanca de direccionales	11. turn signal lever
claxon/bocina	12. horn
eje	13. column
encendido	14. ignition
freno de emergencia	15. emergency brake
asiento deportivo	16. bucket seat
cambio de velocidades/palanca de cambios	17. gearshift
radio	18. radio
tablero	19. dashboard
guantera/gaveta para guantes	20. glove compartment

ventila/ventilador	21. vent
tapete/alfombra	22. mat
cinturón de seguridad	23. seat belt
Transmisión manual	B. Manual Transmission
palanca de velocidades	24. stick shift
clutch/embrague	25. clutch
freno	26. brake
acelerador	27. accelerator
Camioneta	C. Station Wagon
placa/chapa de matrícula/tablilla	28. license plate
luz del freno	29. brake light
luz de reversa	30. back-up light
luz trasera	31. taillight
asiento trasero	32. backseat
asiento para niño	33. child's seat
tanque de gasolina	34. gas tank
respaldo	35. headrest
tapón/tapacubo/tapabocina	36. hubcap
llanta/goma	37. tire

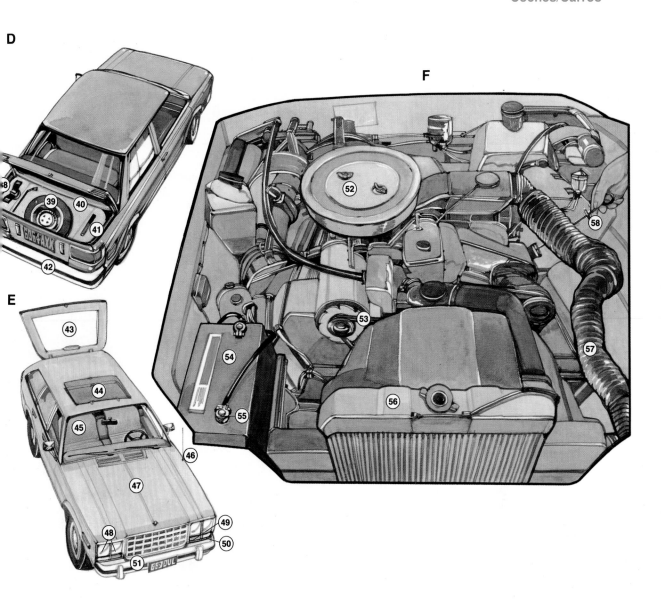

Sedán (dos puertas)	**D. (Two-door) Sedan**	luces delanteras	**48.** headlights
gato	**38.** jack	luces para estacionarse	**49.** parking lights
llanta de repuesto/refacción/repuesta	**39.** spare tire	luces direccionales	**50.** turn signal (lights)
cajuela/maletera/baúl	**40.** trunk	defensa delantera	**51.** front bumper
señal luminosa preventiva	**41.** flare		
defensa trasera	**42.** rear bumper	**Motor**	**F. Engine**
		filtro	**52.** air filter
Camioneta cuatro puertas	**E. Four-door Hatchback**	banda (del ventilador)	**53.** fan belt
compuerta trasera	**43.** hatchback	acumulador/batería	**54.** battery
quemacoco	**44.** sunroof	terminal	**55.** terminal
el parabrisas	**45.** windshield	radiador	**56.** radiator
antena	**46.** antenna	manguera	**57.** hose
toldo/capota	**47.** hood	varilla del aceite	**58.** dipstick

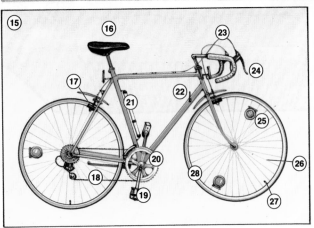

ruedas de entrenamiento	**1.** training wheels		cadena	**18.** chain
manubrios(de carreras)	**2.** (racing) handlebars		pedal	**19.** pedal
bicicleta de mujer	**3.** girl's frame		engrane	**20.** sprocket
rueda	**4.** wheel		pompa	**21.** pump
claxon/bocina	**5.** horn		palanca de velocidades	**22.** gear changer
triciclo	**6.** tricycle		cable	**23.** cable
casco	**7.** helmet		freno manual	**24.** hand brake
bicicleta para campo	**8.** dirt bike		reflector	**25.** reflector
soporte	**9.** kickstand		rayo	**26.** spoke
defensa	**10.** fender		válvula	**27.** valve
bicicleta de hombre	**11.** boy's frame		llanta/goma	**28.** tire
manubrios de viaje	**12.** touring handlebars		moto pequeña	**29.** motor scooter
seguro	**13.** lock		motocicleta	**30.** motorcycle
estante de bicicleta	**14.** bike stand		amortiguadores	**31.** shock absorbers
bicicleta	**15.** bicycle		motor	**32.** engine
asiento	**16.** seat		escape	**33.** exhaust pipe
freno	**17.** brake			

carretera interestatal	**1.** interstate highway
carril de salida	**2.** exit ramp
paso a desnivel	**3.** overpass
cruce de trébol	**4.** cloverleaf
carril izquierdo	**5.** left lane
carril central	**6.** center lane
carril derecho	**7.** right lane
letrero de límite de velocidad	**8.** speed limit sign
persona que viaja pidiendo aventón/ponero	**9.** hitchhiker
casa-remolque	**10.** trailer
área de servicios	**11.** service area
ayudante/asistente	**12.** attendant
bomba de aire/pompa de aire	**13.** air pump
bomba de gasolina/pompa de gasolina	**14.** gas pump
carro de pasajeros	**15.** passenger car
vehículo de remolque para acampar/carro casa	**16.** camper
carro deportivo	**17.** sports car
división central/divisor	**18.** center divider
motocicleta	**19.** motorcycle
autobús	**20.** bus
carril de entrada	**21.** entrance ramp
borde/orilla de la carretera	**22.** shoulder
letrero de carretera	**23.** road sign
letrero de salida	**24.** exit sign
camión	**25.** truck
camión de mudanza	**26.** van
caseta de cobro/peaje	**27.** tollbooth

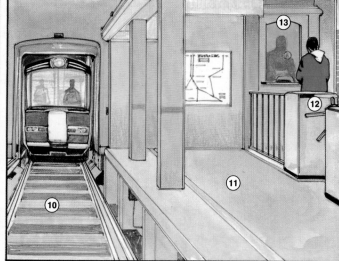

Autobús/Guagua	**A. Bus**
cordón	**1.** cord
asiento	**2.** seat
chofer/conductor	**3.** bus driver
boleto/billete de transbordo	**4.** transfer
alcancía de cuota/tarifa	**5.** fare box
pasajero	**6.** rider

Tren subterráneo/Metro	**B. Subway**
conductor	**7.** conductor
agarradera	**8.** strap
coche/carro de ferrocarril	**9.** car
vía/carril	**10.** track
plataforma	**11.** platform
torniquete de entrada/torno	**12.** turnstile
casilla/taquilla de fichas	**13.** token booth

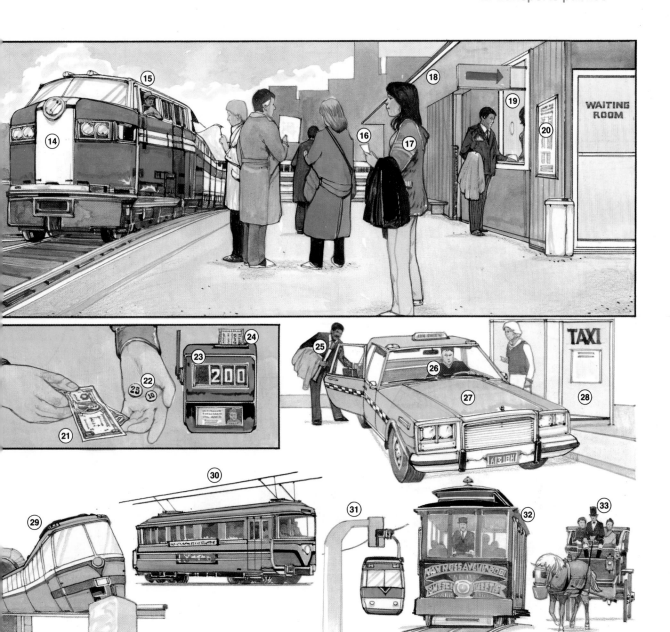

Tren	**C. Train**	recibo	**24.** receipt
tren	**14.** commuter train	pasajero	**25.** passenger
ingeniero	**15.** engineer	taxista	**26.** cab driver
boleto	**16.** ticket	taxi	**27.** taxicab
viajero abonado	**17.** commuter	caseta de taxis	**28.** taxi stand
estación	**18.** station		
taquilla	**19.** ticket window	**Otras formas de transporte**	**E. Other Forms of Transportation**
horario	**20.** timetable		
		monoriel	**29.** monorail
Taxi	**D. Taxi**	tranvía	**30.** streetcar
tarifa/cuota	**21.** fare	tranvía aéreo	**31.** aerial tramway
propina	**22.** tip	tranvía tirado por cable	**32.** cable car
medidor/marcador	**23.** meter	carreta tirada por caballos	**33.** horse-drawn carriage

Registro en el aeropuerto	**Airport Check-In**
porta ropa	**1.** garment bag
bolso de mano	**2.** carry-on bag
viajero	**3.** traveler
boleto/pasaje	**4.** ticket
mozo/maletero	**5.** porter
carrito de equipaje	**6.** dolly
maleta	**7.** suitcase
equipaje	**8.** baggage

Seguridad	**Security**
el guardia de seguridad	**9.** security guard
detector de metales	**10.** metal detector
seleccionador de rayos	**11.** X-ray screener
banda	**12.** conveyor belt

Abordaje	**Boarding**
cabina de mando	**13.** cockpit
instrumentos	**14.** instruments
piloto	**15.** pilot
copiloto	**16.** copilot
ingeniero de vuelo	**17.** flight engineer
pase de abordar	**18.** boarding pass
cabina	**19.** cabin
el, la sobrecargo	**20.** flight attendant
compartimento de equipaje	**21.** luggage compartment
mesita	**22.** tray table
pasillo	**23.** aisle

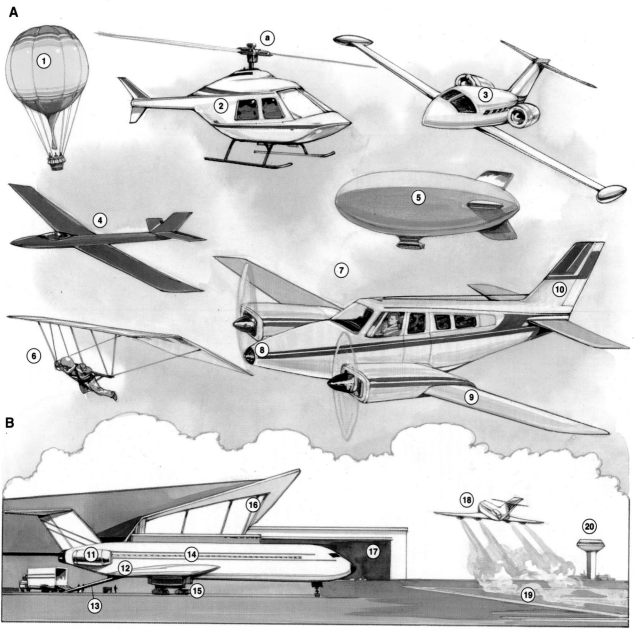

A

B

Clases de aviones	A. Aircraft Types	Despegue	B. Takeoff
globo	**1.** hot air balloon	turbina	**11.** jet engine
helicóptero	**2.** helicopter	el área de carga	**12.** cargo area
hélice	**a.** rotor	puerta de carga	**13.** cargo door
jet privado	**3.** private jet	fuselaje	**14.** fuselage
planeador	**4.** glider	tren de aterrizaje	**15.** landing gear
dirigible	**5.** blimp	la terminal	**16.** terminal building
deslizador	**6.** hang glider	el hangar	**17.** hangar
avión de motor	**7.** propeller plane	el jet	**18.** (jet) plane
trompa (del avión)/nariz	**8.** nose	pista	**19.** runway
ala	**9.** wing	torre de control	**20.** control tower
cola	**10.** tail		

bote de pesca	**1.** fishing boat
pescador	**2.** fisherman
muelle/malecón	**3.** pier
porta carga	**4.** forklift
proa	**5.** bow
grúa	**6.** crane
caja	**7.** container
bodega	**8.** hold
barco de carga	**9.** (container)ship
carga	**10.** cargo
popa	**11.** stern
barcaza/lanchón	**12.** barge
remolcador	**13.** tugboat
faro	**14.** lighthouse
barco tanque	**15.** tanker

boya	**16.** buoy
transbordador	**17.** ferry
chimenea	**18.** smokestack
bote salvavidas	**19.** lifeboat
portalón	**20.** gangway
ventanilla/portilla/clarabolla	**21.** porthole
cubierta	**22.** deck
molinete	**23.** windlass
el ancla	**24.** anchor
cuerda/lazo	**25.** line
bolardo	**26.** bollard
buque (transatlántico)	**27.** ocean liner
dique/desembarcadero	**28.** dock
estación de carga	**29.** terminal

chaleco salvavidas	**1.** life jacket	lancha de motor	**13.** motorboat
canoa	**2.** canoe	deslizador de vela	**14.** windsurfer
remo/paleta (de agua)	**3.** paddle	veleta	**15.** sailboard
bote de vela	**4.** sailboat	bote de paseo	**16.** cabin cruiser
timón	**5.** rudder	canoa de los esquimales	**17.** kayak
orza de deriva/quilla	**6.** centerboard	bote/lancha/botecito	**18.** dinghy
botalón/botavara	**7.** boom	anclaje/bolla	**19.** mooring
mástil	**8.** mast	flotador inflable	**20.** inflatable raft
vela	**9.** sail	escálamo/horquilla	**21.** oarlock
esquiador	**10.** water-skier	remo	**22.** oar
sirga/cuerda de remolque	**11.** towrope	bote de remo	**23.** rowboat
motor exterior	**12.** outboard motor		

Flores	Flowers		gardenia	14. gardenia
tulipán	1. tulip		flor de nochebuena/pascua	15. poinsettia
tallo	**a.** stem		violeta	16. violet
pensamiento	2. pansy		botón de oro	17. buttercup
azucena	3. lily		rosa	18. rose
crisantemo	4. (chrysanthe)mum		botón	**a.** bud
margarita	5. daisy		pétalo	**b.** petal
maravilla/clavelón	6. marigold		espina	**c.** thorn
petunia	7. petunia		girasol	19. sunflower
narciso	8. daffodil			
bulbo	**a.** bulb		**Yerbas y granos**	**Grasses and Grains**
azafrán croco	9. crocus		caña de azúcar	20. sugarcane
jacinto	10. hyacinth		arroz	21. rice
lirio	11. iris		trigo	22. wheat
orquídea	12. orchid		(granos de) avena	23. oats
pompón	13. zinnia		maíz	24. corn

Arboles	**Trees**		olmo	**36.** elm
secoya	**25.** redwood		hoja	**a.** leaf
palmera	**26.** palm		acebo/agrifolio	**37.** holly
eucalipto	**27.** eucalyptus		arce/meple	**38.** maple
cornejo	**28.** dogwood			
magnolia	**29.** magnolia		**Otras plantas**	**Other Plants**
álamo/chopo	**30.** poplar		plantas caseras	**39.** house plants
sauce	**31.** willow		cactus	**40.** cactus
abedul	**32.** birch		arbustos	**41.** bushes
roble	**33.** oak		enredadera	**42.** vine
ramita	**a.** twig			
bellota	**b.** acorn		**Plantas venenosas**	**Poisonous Plants**
pino	**34.** pine		roble venenoso	**43.** poison oak
aguja	**a.** needle		zumaque venenoso	**44.** poison sumac
cono	**b.** cone		hiedra venenosa	**45.** poison ivy
árbol	**35.** tree			
rama	**a.** branch			
tronco	**b.** trunk			
corcho	**c.** bark			
raíz	**d.** root			

caracol	**1.**	snail
concha		**a.** shell
antena		**b.** antenna
ostra	**2.**	oyster
almeja	**3.**	mussel
baboso/babosa	**4.**	slug
calamar	**5.**	squid
pulpo	**6.**	octopus
pez estrella	**7.**	starfish

camarón	**8.**	shrimp
cangrejo/juey	**9.**	crab
escalope/concha	**10.**	scallop
lombriz	**11.**	worm
medusa/aguaviva	**12.**	jellyfish
tentáculo		**a.** tentacle
langosta	**13.**	lobster
pinza/boca		**a.** claw

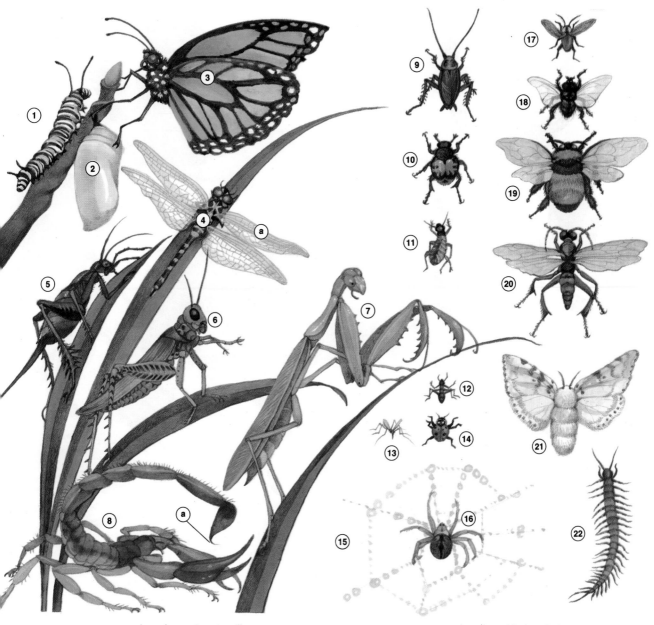

gusano de seda	**1.** caterpillar	termita	**11.** termite
capullo/cocuyo	**2.** cocoon	hormiga	**12.** ant
mariposa	**3.** butterfly	mosquito/zancudo	**13.** mosquito
libélula/caballito de San Pedro	**4.** dragonfly	catarina/mariquita	**14.** ladybug
ala	**a.** wing	telaraña	**15.** web
grillo	**5.** cricket	araña	**16.** spider
chapulín/saltamonte	**6.** grasshopper	luciérnaga/cucubano	**17.** firefly
mantis	**7.** mantis	mosca	**18.** fly
alacrán	**8.** scorpion	abeja	**19.** bee
aguijón	**a.** sting	avispa	**20.** wasp
cucaracha	**9.** cockroach	mariposa nocturna	**21.** moth
escarabajo	**10.** beetle	ciempiés	**22.** centipede

Pájaros/Aves

pichón/paloma	**1.** pigeon		perico/cotorra/loro	**16.** parrot
ala	**a.** wing		pájaro carpintero	**17.** woodpecker
colibrí	**2.** hummingbird		pavo real	**18.** peacock
cuervo	**3.** crow		el faisán	**19.** pheasant
pico	**a.** beak		pavo	**20.** turkey
gaviota	**4.** sea gull		gallo	**21.** rooster
águila	**5.** eagle		pollito	**22.** chick
búho/lechuza	**6.** owl		pollo	**23.** chicken
halcón/falcón	**7.** hawk		pelícano	**24.** pelican
pluma	**a.** feather		pico	**a.** bill
pájaro azul	**8.** blue jay		pato	**25.** duck
petirrojo/pechicolorado	**9.** robin		ganso	**26.** goose
gorrión	**10.** sparrow		pingüino	**27.** penguin
cardenal	**11.** cardinal		cisne	**28.** swan
el avestruz	**12.** ostrich		flamingo	**29.** flamingo
huevo	**13.** egg		cigüeña	**30.** stork
canario	**14.** canary		nido	**31.** nest
periquito	**15.** parakeet		correcaminos	**32.** roadrunner

Peces	**A. Fish**		Anfibios y reptiles	**B. Amphibians and Reptiles**
caballo de mar	**1.** sea horse		cocodrilo	**8.** alligator
trucha	**2.** trout		culebra/víbora	**9.** (garter) snake
pez espada	**3.** swordfish		víbora de cascabel	**10.** rattlesnake
cola	**a.** tail		cobra	**11.** cobra
aleta	**b.** fin		tortuga	**12.** turtle
agalla	**c.** gill		iguana	**13.** iguana
anguila	**4.** eel		salamandra	**14.** salamander
tiburón	**5.** shark		lagartija	**15.** lizard
mantaraya	**6.** stingray		renacuajo/ajolote	**16.** tadpole
robalo/mojarra	**7.** flounder		rana	**17.** frog
			tortuga gigante	**18.** tortoise
			concha/carapacho	**a.** shell

Mamíferos de bolsa, sin dientes, y voladores	**Pouched, Toothless, or Flying Mammals**
(oso) koala	**1.** koala
armadillo	**2.** armadillo
canguro	**3.** kangaroo
cola	**a.** tail
patas traseras	**b.** hind legs
bolsa	**c.** pouch
patas frontales	**d.** forelegs
murciélago	**4.** bat
oso hormiguero	**5.** anteater
Roedores	**Rodents**
ardillita	**6.** chipmunk
rata	**7.** rat
topo	**8.** gopher

ratón	**9.** mouse
ardilla	**10.** squirrel
puerco espín	**11.** porcupine
púa	**a.** quill
castor	**12.** beaver
conejo	**13.** rabbit
Mamíferos de pezuña	**Hoofed Mammals**
hipopótamo	**14.** hippopotamus
llama	**15.** llama
rinoceronte	**16.** rhinoceros
cuerno	**a.** horn
elefante	**17.** elephant
trompa	**a.** trunk
colmillo	**b.** tusk
cebra	**18.** zebra

bisonte	**19.** bison		girafa	**29.** giraffe
pony	**20.** pony		cerdo	**30.** hog
caballo	**21.** horse		becerro/ternero	**31.** calf
crin de caballo	**a.** mane		vaca	**32.** cow
potro	**22.** foal		camello	**33.** camel
burro	**23.** donkey		joroba	**a.** hump
borrego/oveja pequeña	**24.** lamb		toro	**34.** bull
cordero/oveja	**25.** sheep		alce	**35.** moose
venado	**26.** deer		cuerno/asta	**a.** antler
cervato/venadito	**27.** fawn		pezuña	**b.** hoof
chivo	**28.** goat			

leopardo	**1.** leopard	**Mamíferos acuáticos**	**Aquatic Mammals**
tigre	**2.** tiger	ballena	**9.** whale
garra	**a.** claw	nutria	**10.** otter
león	**3.** lion	morsa	**11.** walrus
gato	**4.** cat	foca	**12.** seal
gatito	**5.** kitten	pata de foca	**a.** flipper
zorro	**6.** fox	delfín	**13.** dolphin
mapache	**7.** raccoon		
zorrillo	**8.** skunk		

Primates	Primates
chango/mico	**14.** monkey
mono de Asia	**15.** gibbon
chimpancé	**16.** chimpanzee
gorila	**17.** gorilla
orangután	**18.** orangutan
mandril	**19.** baboon

Osos	Bears
oso panda	**20.** panda
oso negro	**21.** black bear
oso polar	**22.** polar bear
oso pardo	**23.** grizzly bear

Perros	Dogs
spaniel/perro de aguas	**24.** spaniel
terrier	**25.** terrier
perro cobrador	**26.** retriever
cachorro	**27.** puppy
pastor	**28.** shepherd
lobo	**29.** wolf
pata/garra	**a.** paw
hiena	**30.** hyena

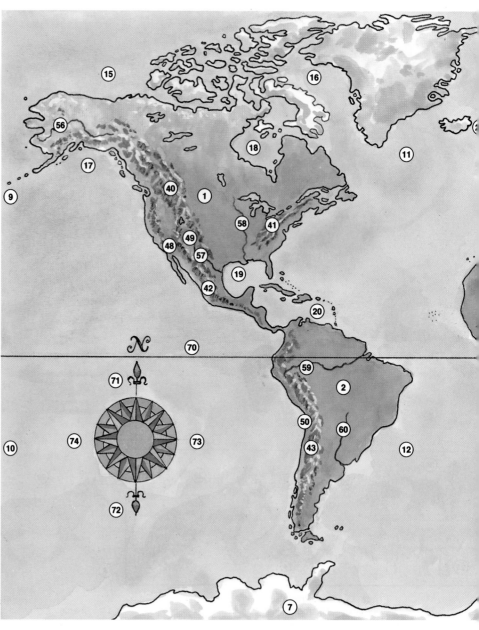

Continentes	Continents
Norteamérica	**1.** North America
Sudamérica	**2.** South America
Europa	**3.** Europe
Africa	**4.** Africa
Asia	**5.** Asia
Australia	**6.** Australia
Antártica	**7.** Antarctica

Océanos	Oceans
Artico	**8.** Arctic
Pacífico del norte	**9.** North Pacific
Pacífico del sur	**10.** South Pacific
Atlántico del norte	**11.** North Atlantic
Atlántico del sur	**12.** South Atlantic
Indico	**13.** Indian
Antártico	**14.** Antarctic

Mares, golfos y bahías	Seas, Gulfs, and Bays
Mar de Beaufort	**15.** Beaufort Sea
Bahía Baffin	**16.** Baffin Bay
Golfo de Alaska	**17.** Gulf of Alaska
Bahía del Hudson	**18.** Hudson Bay
Golfo de México	**19.** Gulf of Mexico
Mar del Caribe/Mar Caribe	**20.** Caribbean Sea
Mar del Norte	**21.** North Sea
Mar Báltico	**22.** Baltic Sea
Mar de Barents	**23.** Barents Sea
Mar Mediterráneo	**24.** Mediterranean Sea
Golfo de Guinea	**25.** Gulf of Guinea
Mar Negro	**26.** Black Sea
Mar Caspiano	**27.** Caspian Sea
Golfo Pérsico	**28.** Persian Gulf
Mar Rojo	**29.** Red Sea

Mar Arábigo	**30.** Arabian Sea
Mar de Kara	**31.** Kara Sea
Bahía de Bengala	**32.** Bay of Beng
Mar de Laptev	**33.** Laptev Sea
Mar de Bering	**34.** Bering Sea
Mar de Okhotsk	**35.** Sea of Okh
Mar del Japón	**36.** Sea of Japa
Mar Amarillo	**37.** Yellow Sea
Mar del Este de China	**38.** East China
Mar del Sur de China	**39.** South China

Cordilleras	Mountain Ranges		Rubalcali	52. Rub' al Khali	Yenisey	65. Yenisey
Montañas Rocallosas	40. Rocky Mountains		Takla Makan	53. Takla Makan	Lena	66. Lena
ntañas Apalaches/Montes	41. Appalachian Mountains		Gobi	54. Gobi	Ganges	67. Ganges
Apalaches			Arenoso	55. Great Sandy	Huang	68. Huang
Sierra Madre	42. Sierra Madre				Yangtzé	69. Yangtze
Andes	43. Andes		**Ríos**	**Rivers**		
Alpes	44. Alps		Yukón	56. Yukon	ecuador	70. equator
Montañas Cáucaso	45. Caucasus		Río Grande	57. Rio Grande	norte	71. north
Montes Urales	46. Urals		Misisipí	58. Mississippi	sur	72. south
Himalayas	47. Himalayas		Amazonas	59. Amazon	este	73. east
			Paraná	60. Paraná	oeste	74. west
Desiertos	**Deserts**		Níger	61. Niger		
Mojave	48. Mojave		Congo	62. Congo		
Pintado	49. Painted		Nilo	63. Nile		
Atacama	50. Atacama		Ob	64. Ob		
Sahara	51. Sahara					

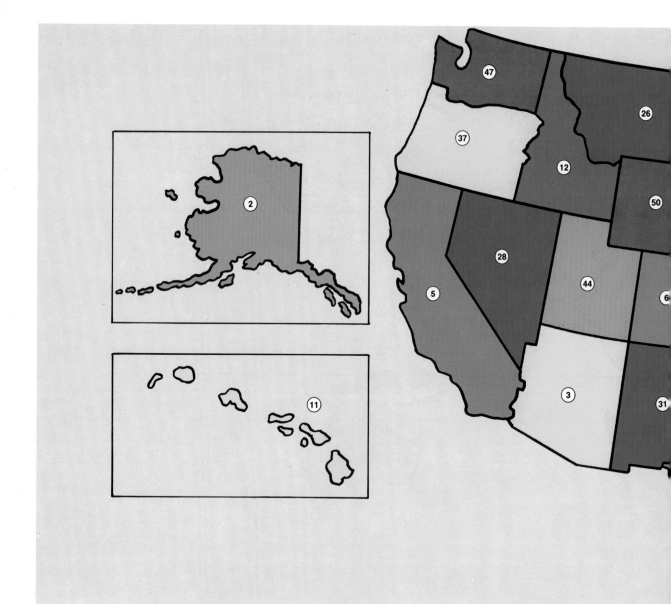

Alabama	**1.** Alabama	Illinois	**13.** Illinois
Alaska	**2.** Alaska	Indiana	**14.** Indiana
Arizona	**3.** Arizona	Iowa	**15.** Iowa
Arkansas	**4.** Arkansas	Kansas	**16.** Kansas
California	**5.** California	Kentucky	**17.** Kentucky
Colorado	**6.** Colorado	Louisiana	**18.** Louisiana
Connecticut	**7.** Connecticut	Maine	**19.** Maine
Delaware	**8.** Delaware	Maryland	**20.** Maryland
Florida	**9.** Florida	Massachusetts	**21.** Massachusetts
Georgia	**10.** Georgia	Michigan	**22.** Michigan
Hawaii	**11.** Hawaii	Minnesota	**23.** Minnesota
Idaho	**12.** Idaho	Misisipi	**24.** Mississippi

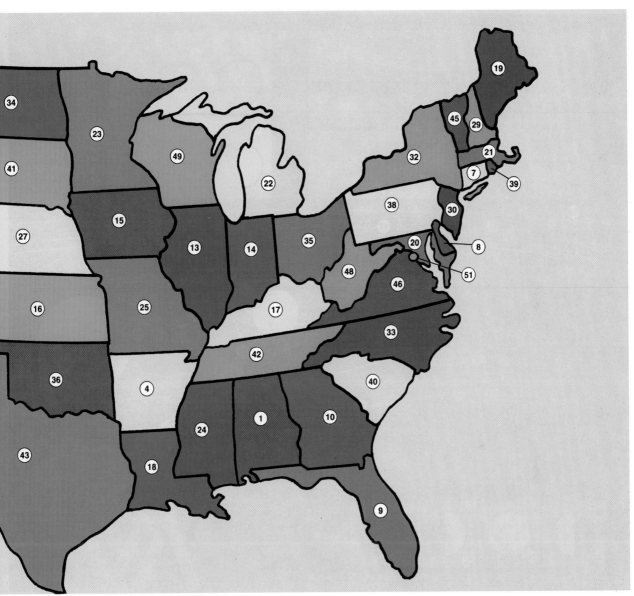

Missouri	**25.** Missouri		Rhode Island	**39.** Rhode Island
Montana	**26.** Montana		Carolina del sur	**40.** South Carolina
Nebraska	**27.** Nebraska		Dakota del sur	**41.** South Dakota
Nevada	**28.** Nevada		Tennessee	**42.** Tennessee
Nueva Hampshire	**29.** New Hampshire		Texas	**43.** Texas
Nueva Jersey	**30.** New Jersey		Utah	**44.** Utah
Nuevo México	**31.** New Mexico		Vermont	**45.** Vermont
Nueva York	**32.** New York		Virginia	**46.** Virginia
Carolina del norte	**33.** North Carolina		Washington	**47.** Washington
Dakota del norte	**34.** North Dakota		West Virginia	**48.** West Virginia
Ohio	**35.** Ohio		Wisconsin	**49.** Wisconsin
Oklahoma	**36.** Oklahoma		Wyoming	**50.** Wyoming
Oregon	**37.** Oregon			
Pennsylvania	**38.** Pennsylvania		Distrito de Columbia	**51.** District of Columbia

Espacio exterior	**A. Outer Space**
galaxia	**1.** galaxy
cometa	**2.** comet
constelación (Osa Mayor)	**3.** (Big Dipper) constellation
estrella	**4.** star
meteoro	**5.** meteor
El Sistema Solar	**B. The Solar System**
eclipse lunar	**6.** lunar eclipse
sol	**7.** Sun
tierra	**8.** Earth
luna	**9.** Moon
eclipse solar	**10.** solar eclipse
Los Planetas	*The Planets*
Mercurio	**11.** Mercury
Venus	**12.** Venus
Tierra	**13.** Earth

Marte	**14.** Mars
Júpiter	**15.** Jupiter
Saturno	**16.** Saturn
anillo	**a.** ring
Urano	**17.** Uranus
Neptuno	**18.** Neptune
Plutón	**19.** Pluto
asteroide	**20.** asteroid
órbita	**21.** orbit
telescopio	**22.** telescope
Fases de la luna	**C. Phases of the Moon**
primer cuarto	**23.** first quarter
luna llena	**24.** full moon
cuarto menguante	**25.** last quarter
luna nueva	**26.** new moon

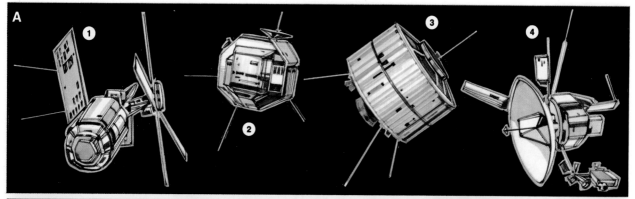

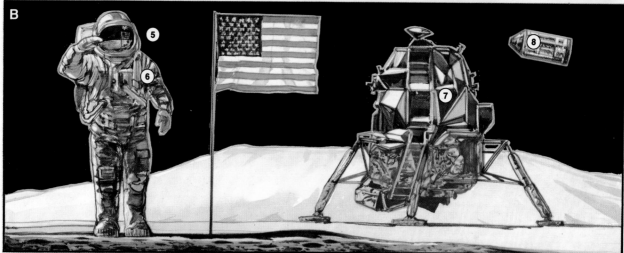

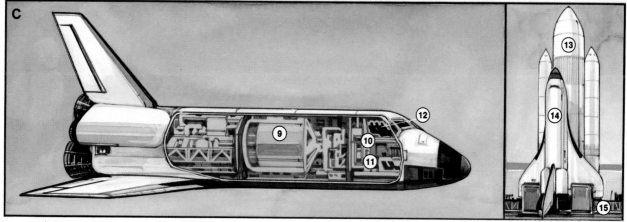

Naves espaciales	A. Spacecraft	El transbordador espacial	C. The Space Shuttle
estación espacial	1. space station	sección de carga	9. cargo bay
satélite de comunicación	2. communication satellite	cubierta de vuelo	10. flight deck
satélite climatológico	3. weather satellite	área habitacional	11. living quarters
explorador espacial	4. space probe	tripulación	12. crew
		cohete	13. rocket
Alunizaje	B. Landing on the Moon	transbordador espacial	14. space shuttle
astronauta	5. astronaut	plataforma de despegue	15. launchpad
traje espacial	6. space suit		
módulo lunar	7. lunar module		
módulo de comando	8. command module		

bandera	**1.** flag	cuaderno de espiral	**15.** spiral notebook
reloj	**2.** clock	escritorio	**16.** desk
bocina/altoparlante	**3.** loudspeaker	pegamento/pega	**17.** glue
maestra	**4.** teacher	brocha	**18.** brush
pizarrón/pizarra	**5.** chalkboard	el, la estudiante	**19.** student
armario/locker	**6.** locker	sacapuntas	**20.** pencil sharpener
tablero de anuncios/tablón de edictos	**7.** bulletin board	borrador/goma	**21.** pencil eraser
		pluma atómica/bolígrafo	**22.** ballpoint pen
computadora	**8.** computer	regla	**23.** ruler
repisa del gis/canal de tizas	**9.** chalk tray	lápiz	**24.** pencil
gis/tiza	**10.** chalk	tachuela	**25.** thumbtack
borrador	**11.** eraser	libro (de texto)	**26.** (text)book
pasillo	**12.** hall	retroproyector	**27.** overhead projector
(hojas sueltas de) papel	**13.** (loose-leaf) paper		
carpeta	**14.** ring binder		

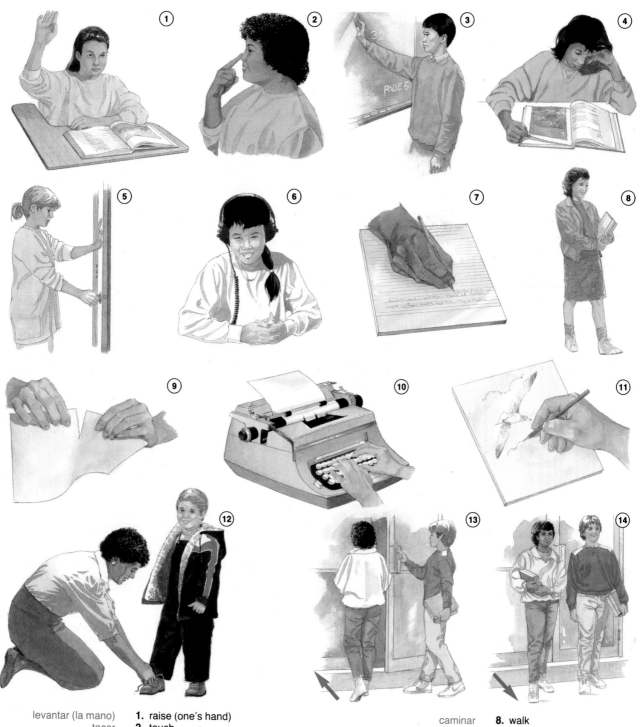

levantar (la mano)	**1.** raise (one's hand)
tocar	**2.** touch
borrar	**3.** erase
leer	**4.** read
cerrar	**5.** close
escuchar	**6.** listen
escribir	**7.** write

caminar	**8.** walk
romper/rasgar	**9.** tear
escribir a máquina	**10.** type
dibujar	**11.** draw
amarrar	**12.** tie
salir	**13.** leave
entrar	**14.** enter

prisma	**1.** prism		tubo de hule/goma	**18.** rubber tubing
frasco	**2.** flask		soporte del aro	**19.** ring stand
platito de muestras	**3.** petri dish		quemador	**20.** Bunsen burner
escala/pesa balanza	**4.** scale		flama	**21.** flame
pesas	**5.** weights		termómetro	**22.** thermometer
red metálica	**6.** wire mesh screen		tazón	**23.** beaker
tornillo	**7.** clamp		mesa de trabajo	**24.** bench
estante	**8.** rack		cilindro graduado	**25.** graduated cylinder
proveta	**9.** test tube		gotero	**26.** medicine dropper
tapón	**10.** stopper		imán	**27.** magnet
papel de gráficas/gráfico	**11.** graph paper		tenazas/pinzas	**28.** forceps
lentes de seguridad	**12.** safety glasses		pinzas	**29.** tongs
medidor de tiempo	**13.** timer		microscopio	**30.** microscope
popote/tubo de vidrio	**14.** pipette		muestra en transparencia	**31.** slide
lupa	**15.** magnifying glass		pincitas/tenacillas	**32.** tweezers
papel filtro	**16.** filter paper		estuche de disección	**33.** dissection kit
embudo	**17.** funnel		banco	**34.** stool

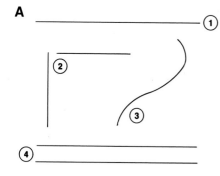

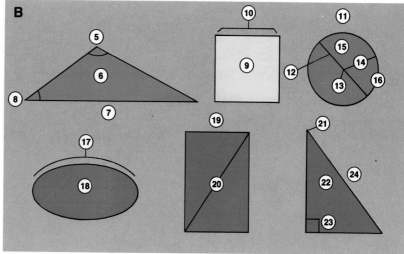

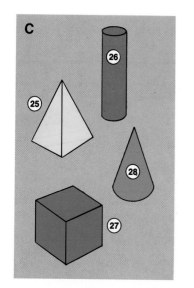

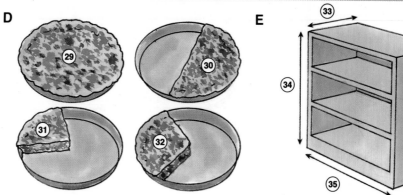

Líneas	**A. Lines**
línea recta	**1.** straight line
líneas perpendiculares	**2.** perpendicular lines
curva	**3.** curve
líneas paralelas	**4.** parallel lines

Figuras geométricas	**B. Geometrical Figures**
ángulo obtuso	**5.** obtuse angle
triángulo	**6.** triangle
base	**7.** base
ángulo agudo	**8.** acute angle
cuadrado	**9.** square
lado	**10.** side
círculo	**11.** circle
diámetro	**12.** diameter
centro	**13.** center
radio	**14.** radius
sección	**15.** section
arco	**16.** arc
circunferencia	**17.** circumference
óvalo	**18.** oval
rectángulo	**19.** rectangle
diagonal	**20.** diagonal

ápice/cumbre	**21.** apex
triángulo recto	**22.** right triangle
ángulo recto	**23.** right angle
hipotenusa	**24.** hypotenuse

Figuras sólidas	**C. Solid Figures**
pirámide	**25.** pyramid
cilindro	**26.** cylinder
cubo	**27.** cube
cono	**28.** cone

Fracciones	**D. Fractions**
entero	**29.** whole
un medio	**30.** a half (1/2)
un cuarto	**31.** a quarter (1/4)
un tercio	**32.** a third (1/3)

Medidas	**E. Measurement**
profundidad	**33.** depth
altura	**34.** height
ancho	**35.** width
largo	**36.** length

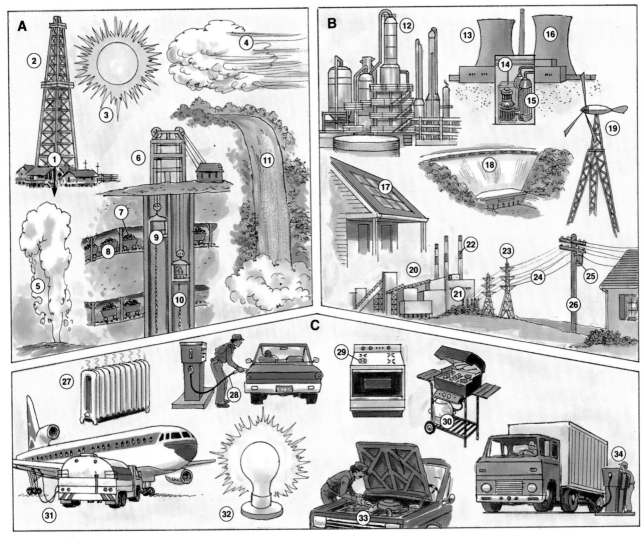

Fuentes de fuerza/energía	**A. Sources of Power**
pozo petrolero	**1.** oil well
armazón	**2.** derrick
sol	**3.** sun
viento	**4.** wind
geyser	**5.** geyser
mina de carbón	**6.** coal mine
carbón	**7.** coal
vagón transportador	**8.** shuttle car
elevador	**9.** elevator
(pozo) tiro de elevador	**10.** shaft
cascada/caída de agua	**11.** waterfall

Producción de energía	**B. Generation of Power**
refinería	**12.** refinery
reactor nuclear	**13.** nuclear reactor
núcleo	**14.** core
varillas de uranio	**15.** uranium rods
torre enfriadora	**16.** cooling tower
colector solar	**17.** solar collector

presa	**18.** dam
molino de viento	**19.** windmill
casa de fuerza/casa de energía	**20.** power station
generador eléctrico	**21.** electrical generator
chimenea	**22.** smokestack
torres transmisoras	**23.** transmission towers
líneas de corriente/energía	**24.** power lines
transformador	**25.** transformer
poste de servicio	**26.** utility pole

Usos y productos	**C. Uses and Products**
calefacción	**27.** heat
gasolina	**28.** gas(oline)
gas natural	**29.** natural gas
gas propano	**30.** propane gas
combustible para jet	**31.** jet fuel
electricidad	**32.** electricity
aceite de motor	**33.** motor oil
combustible diesel	**34.** diesel fuel

Granja lechera	A. Dairy Farm
huerta	1. orchard
árbol frutal	2. fruit tree
casa de granja	3. farmhouse
silo	4. silo
granero	5. barn
pastura/pastisal	6. pasture
granjero	7. farmer
corral	8. barnyard
cerca	9. fence
borregos/ovejas	10. sheep
vaca lechera	11. dairy cow
Granja de trigo	B. Wheat Farm
ganado	12. livestock
(bulto de) paja/(mazo de) paja	13. (bale of) hay

trinche	14. pitchfork
tractor	15. tractor
trigal	16. (wheat) field
segadora trilladora	17. combine
surco/fila	18. row
espantapájaros	19. scarecrow
Rancho	C. Ranch
(manada de) ganado	20. (herd of) cattle
vaquero	21. cowboy
vaquera	22. cowgirl
caballos	23. horses
corral	24. corral
bebedero	25. trough

Local de construcción	A. Construction Site		pala	15. shovel
vigas	1. rafters		tabla	16. board
tejas	2. shingle		operario que repara la línea	17. linesman
nivel	3. level		grúa con plataforma movible	18. cherry picker
sombrero duro/casco	4. hard hat			
constructor	5. builder		**Trabajo en carretera**	**B. Road Work**
planos	6. blueprints		cono preventivo	19. cone
andamiaje	7. scaffolding		banderín	20. flag
escalera	8. ladder		barricada	21. barricade
escalón	9. rung		martillo perforador	22. jackhammer
cemento	10. cement		carretilla	23. wheelbarrow
cimiento	11. foundation		muro central/divisorio	24. center divider
ladrillos	12. bricks		mezcladora de cemento	25. cement mixer
pico	13. pickax		pala mecánica	26. backhoe
trabajador de construcción	14. construction worker		excavadora	27. bulldozer

operadora de conmutador	**1.** switchboard operator	silla de mecanógrafa	**17.** typing chair
auriculares/audífonos	**2.** headset	gerente	**18.** manager
conmutador	**3.** switchboard	calculadora	**19.** calculator
impresora	**4.** printer	librero	**20.** bookcase
cubículo	**5.** cubicle	archivero	**21.** file cabinet
mecanógrafa	**6.** typist	archivo	**22.** file folder
procesador de palabras	**7.** word processor	archivista	**23.** file clerk
listado	**8.** printout	fotocopiadora	**24.** photocopier
calendario	**9.** calendar	block para mensajes	**25.** message pad
máquina de escribir	**10.** typewriter	block (de papel)	**26.** (legal) pad
secretaria	**11.** secretary	engrapadora/grapadora	**27.** stapler
documentación recibida	**12.** in-box	sujeta papel	**28.** paper clips
escritorio	**13.** desk	desengrapador/uña	**29.** staple remover
rolodex	**14.** rolodex	sacapuntas	**30.** pencil sharpener
teléfono	**15.** telephone	sobre	**31.** envelope
computadora	**16.** computer		

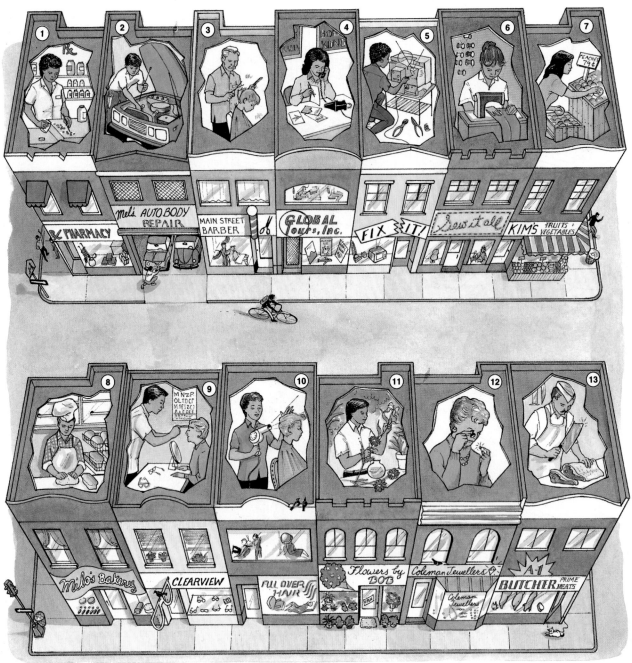

farmacéutica/farmaceuta	**1.** pharmacist
mecánico	**2.** mechanic
peluquero	**3.** barber
agente de viajes	**4.** travel agent
técnica en reparación	**5.** repairperson
costurera/sastre	**6.** tailor
verdulera	**7.** greengrocer

panadero	**8.** baker
el, la oculista/óptico	**9.** optician
el, la estilista	**10.** hairdresser
el florista	**11.** florist
joyera	**12.** jeweller
carnicero	**13.** butcher

Reparación y mantenimiento	A. Repair and Maintenance
plomera	1. plumber
carpintero	2. carpenter
jardinero	3. gardener
cerrajero	4. locksmith
agente de bienes raíces	5. real estate agent
el, la electricista	6. electrician
pintora	7. painter

Servicios domésticos	B. Household Services
ama de llaves	8. housekeeper
empleado de limpieza	9. janitor
mensajero	10. delivery boy
portero	11. doorman

Trabajo en fábrica	C. Factory Work
operario	12. shop worker
el, la capataz	13. foreman

Medios de comunicación y las artes	**A. Media and Arts**
pronosticador del tiempo	**1.** weather forecaster
locutor de noticiero	**2.** newscaster
el, la artista	**3.** artist
fotógrafo	**4.** photographer
el, la modelo	**5.** model
diseñador de moda	**6.** fashion designer
escritor	**7.** writer
arquitecto	**8.** architect
disc jockey	**9.** disc jockey (DJ)
camarógrafo	**10.** cameraperson
reportero	**11.** reporter
vendedor(a)	**12.** salesperson

Transacciones bancarias	**B. Banking**
oficial	**13.** officer
guardia de seguridad	**14.** security guard
cajero	**15.** teller
Empleados de negocios	**C. Business Workers**
programador (de computadora)	**16.** computer programmer
el, la recepcionista	**17.** receptionist
contador	**18.** accountant
mensajero/mandadero	**19.** messenger

zoológico	**1.** zoo		basurero/zafacón	**11.** trash can
teatro al aire libre	**2.** band shell		resbaladilla/chorrera	**12.** slide
vendedor	**3.** vendor		cajón de arena	**13.** sandbox
carrito manual	**4.** hand truck		rociador/chorrito	**14.** sprinkler
caballitos	**5.** merry-go-round		área de juego/parque	**15.** playground
caballista	**6.** horseback rider		columpios	**16.** swings
camino de harradura	**7.** bridle path		juegos infantiles	**17.** jungle gym
estanque (de patos)	**8.** (duck) pond		subibaja	**18.** seesaw
pista para correr	**9.** jogging path		bebedero/fuente	**19.** water fountain
banca	**10.** bench			

meseta	**1.** plateau
excursionistas	**2.** hikers
cañón	**3.** canyon
colina	**4.** hill
el, la guarda parques/guarda bosques	**5.** park ranger

Pesca	**Fishing**
arroyuelo	**6.** stream
caña de pesca	**7.** fishing rod
cordón de pesca	**8.** fishing line
red de pesca	**9.** fishing net
botas/pantalones impermeables para pescar	**10.** waders
rocas	**11.** rocks

Area de picnic	**Picnic Area**
parrilla	**12.** grill
canasta de día de campo	**13.** picnic basket
termo	**14.** thermos
mesa de día de campo	**15.** picnic table

Viajando en balsa	**Rafting**
balsa	**16.** raft
rápidos de río	**17.** rapids
cascada	**18.** waterfall

Alpinismo	**Mountain Climbing**
montaña	**19.** mountain
pico	**20.** peak
barranca	**21.** cliff
guarniciones/aparejo	**22.** harness
cuerda/soga	**23.** rope

Acampando	**Camping**
casa de campaña	**24.** tent
estufa de campamento	**25.** camp stove
bolsa para dormir	**26.** sleeping bag
equipo (de alpinismo)	**27.** gear
mochila con armazón	**28.** frame backpack
linterna/lámpara	**29.** lantern
estaca	**30.** stake
fogata	**31.** campfire
bosques	**32.** woods

camino entarimado/entablado	**1.** boardwalk
puesto de refrescos	**2.** refreshment stand
motel	**3.** motel
ciclista	**4.** biker
silbato	**5.** whistle
el, la salvavidas (persona)	**6.** lifeguard
binoculares/gemelos	**7.** binoculars
silla del salvavidas	**8.** lifeguard chair
salvavidas (objeto)	**9.** life preserver
bote salvavidas	**10.** lifeboat
pelota de playa	**11.** beach ball

dunas de arena	**12.** sand dunes
frisbee/platillo	**13.** Frisbee ™
lentes para el sol/gafas de sol	**14.** sunglasses
toalla de playa	**15.** beach towel
cubeta/cubito/balde	**16.** pail
pala	**17.** shovel
traje de baño	**18.** bathing suit
el, la bañista	**19.** sunbather
silla de playa	**20.** beach chair
parasol/sombrilla de playa	**21.** beach umbrella

cometa/papalote/chiringa	**22.** kite		castillo de arena	**32.** sandcastle
corredores	**23.** runners		shorts de baño	**33.** bathing trunks
ola	**24.** wave		respirador	**34.** snorkel
planeador de mar/tabla	**25.** surfboard		visor/careta	**35.** mask
colchón de aire	**26.** air mattress		aletas/chapaletas	**36.** flippers
planeador pequeño de agua	**27.** kickboard		tanque de oxígeno	**37.** scuba tank
nadador	**28.** swimmer		traje de buceo	**38.** wet suit
llanta inflable/tubo	**29.** tube		loción para el sol	**39.** suntan lotion
agua	**30.** water		concha/caracol	**40.** shell
arena	**31.** sand		hielera/nevera	**41.** cooler

Béisbol	**Baseball**
árbitro	**1.** umpire
cácher/receptor	**2.** catcher
máscara del cácher	**3.** catcher's mask
guante del cácher	**4.** catcher's mitt
bate	**5.** bat
casco del bateador	**6.** batting helmet
bateador	**7.** batter

Pequeña Liga de béisbol	**Little League Baseball**
pequeño jugador de liga	**8.** Little Leaguer
uniforme	**9.** uniform

Softball	**Softball**
pelota de softball	**10.** softball
gorra	**11.** cap
guante	**12.** glove

Fútbol	**Football**
fútbol	**13.** football
casco	**14.** helmet

Lacrosse	**Lacrosse**
careta	**15.** face guard
raqueta de lacrosse	**16.** lacrosse stick

Hockey sobre hielo	**Ice Hockey**
disco de (hule duro) hockey	**17.** puck
palo de hockey	**18.** hockey stick

Baloncesto	**Basketball**
tablero	**19.** backboard
canasta	**20.** basket
balón	**21.** basketball

Vólibol	**Volleyball**
vólibol	**22.** volleyball
red	**23.** net

Fútbol	**Soccer**
portero	**24.** goalie
gol	**25.** goal
balón	26. soccer ball

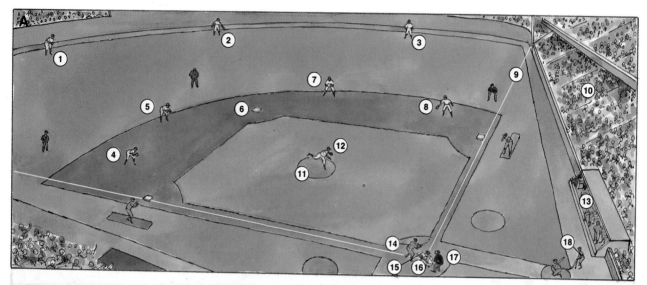

Diamante de béisbol	**A. Baseball Diamond**
campista izquierdo	**1.** left fielder
campista central	**2.** center fielder
campista derecho	**3.** right fielder
tercera base	**4.** third baseman
campo/campista delantero	**5.** shortstop
base	**6.** base
segunda base	**7.** second baseman
primera base	**8.** first baseman
línea de fuera	**9.** foul line
tribunas	**10.** stands
montículo	**11.** pitcher's mound
lanzador	**12.** pitcher
banco	**13.** dugout
bateador	**14.** batter
base	**15.** home plate
cácher/receptor	**16.** catcher
árbitro	**17.** umpire
muchacho de los bates	**18.** batboy

Campo de fútbol	**B. Football Field**
tablero (de puntuación/puntaje)	**19.** scoreboard
porristas	**20.** cheerleaders
entrenador	**21.** coach
árbitro	**22.** referee
zona de gol	**23.** end zone
ala/extremo	**24.** split end
atajador izquierdo	**25.** left tackle
defensa izquierdo	**26.** left guard
centro	**27.** center
defensa derecho	**28.** right guard
atajador derecho	**29.** right tackle
ala extrema	**30.** tight end
flanqueador	**31.** flanker
mariscal de campo	**32.** quarterback
medio trasero	**33.** halfback
trasero	**34.** fullback
poste del gol	**35.** goalpost

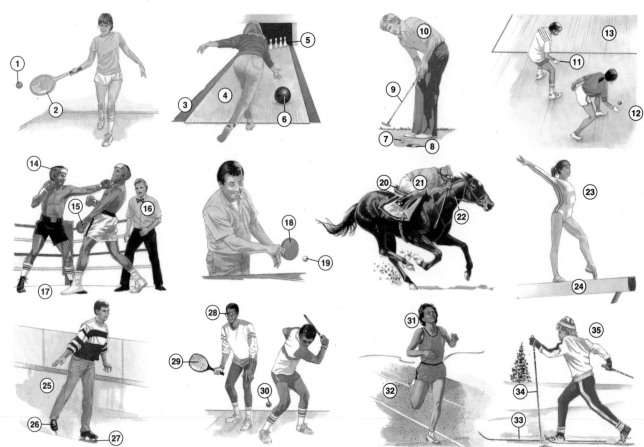

Tenis	Tennis
bola de tenis	1. tennis ball
raqueta	2. racket

Boliche/Bolos — **Bowling**
- canal — 3. gutter
- carril — 4. lane
- pino/bolo — 5. pin
- bola de boliche — 6. bowling ball

Golf — **Golf**
- bola de golf — 7. golf ball
- hoyo — 8. hole
- palo — 9. putter
- golfista — 10. golfer

Frontón de mano — **Handball**
- guante — 11. glove
- bola de frontón — 12. handball
- cancha — 13. court

Boxeo — **Boxing**
- casco protector — 14. head protector
- guante — 15. glove
- árbitro — 16. referee
- cuadrilátero — 17. ring

Ping-pong — **Ping-Pong**
- raqueta/paleta — 18. paddle
- bola de ping-pong — 19. ping-pong ball

Carreras de caballo — **Horse Racing**
- silla de montar — 20. saddle
- jockey/jinete (profesional) — 21. jockey
- riendas — 22. reins

Gimnasia — **Gymnastics**
- el, la gimnasta — 23. gymnast
- barra de balance — 24. balance beam

Patinaje en hielo — **Ice Skating**
- pista — 25. rink
- patín — 26. skate
- hoja/navaja — 27. blade

Frontón con raqueta — **Racquetball**
- lentes de protección — 28. safety goggles
- raqueta — 29. racquet
- bola de frontón con raqueta — 30. racquetball

Atletismo — **Track and Field**
- corredor — 31. runner
- pista — 32. track

Esquiando a campo traviesa — **Cross-Country Skiing**
- esquíes — 33. skis
- palo largo — 34. pole
- esquiador — 35. skier

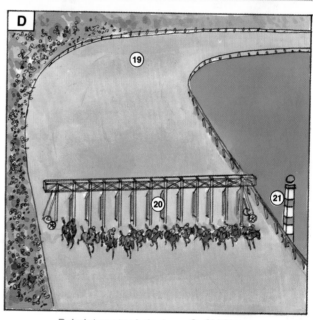

Cancha de tenis	**A. Tennis Court**
sección del saque	**1.** service court
red	**2.** net
línea del saque	**3.** service line
línea de fuera	**4.** baseline

Campo de golf	**B. Golf Course**
palos de golf	**5.** clubs
escabroso	**6.** rough
bolsa de golf	**7.** golf bag
carrito de golf	**8.** golf cart
bandera/banderín	**9.** flag
área verde	**10.** green
trampa de arena	**11.** sand trap
área verde y plana	**12.** fairway
portabola	**13.** tee

Bajada/cuesta abajo de esquiar	**C. Ski Slope**
palo largo	**14.** pole
bota de esquiar	**15.** ski boot
ribete	**16.** binding
esquí	**17.** ski
ascensor de esquíes	**18.** ski lift

Pista de carreras	**D. Race Track**
trecho	**19.** stretch
puerta de salida	**20.** starting gate
meta	**21.** finish line

pegar/golpear	**1.** hit
servir	**2.** serve
patear	**3.** kick
cachar/agarrar	**4.** catch

pasar	**5.** pass
correr	**6.** run
caer	**7.** fall
brincar	**8.** jump

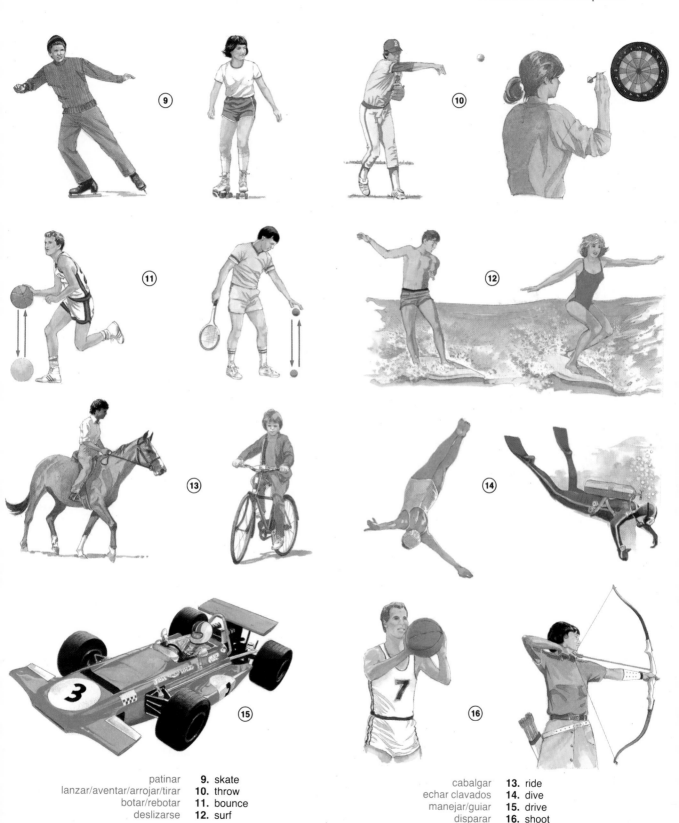

patinar	**9.** skate
lanzar/aventar/arrojar/tirar	**10.** throw
botar/rebotar	**11.** bounce
deslizarse	**12.** surf

cabalgar	**13.** ride
echar clavados	**14.** dive
manejar/guiar	**15.** drive
disparar	**16.** shoot

Instrumentos de cuerdas   **Strings**

piano   **1.** piano
teclado   **a.** keyboard
hoja de música   **2.** sheet music
ukulele   **3.** ukulele
mandolina   **4.** mandolin
banjo   **5.** banjo
harpa   **6.** harp
violín   **7.** violin
arco   **a.** bow
viola   **8.** viola
cello   **9.** cello
bajo   **10.** bass
cuerda   **a.** string
guitarra   **11.** guitar
uñero/uña   **a.** pick

Instrumentos de viento   **Woodwinds**

picolo   **12.** piccolo
flauta   **13.** flute
fagot, bajón   **14.** bassoon
oboe   **15.** oboe
clarinete   **16.** clarinet

Instrumentos de percusión   **Percussion**

tamborina/pandereta   **17.** tambourine
platillos   **18.** cymbals
tambor   **19.** drum
palitos/bolillos, de tambor   **a.** drumsticks
conga   **20.** conga
tambora/timbal   **21.** kettledrum
bongos   **22.** bongos

Instrumentos de metal   **Brass**

trombón   **23.** trombone
saxofón   **24.** saxophone
trompeta   **25.** trumpet
corneta francesa   **26.** French horn
tuba   **27.** tuba

Otros instrumentos   **Other Instruments**

acordeón   **28.** accordion
órgano   **29.** organ
harmónica   **30.** harmonica
xilófono   **31.** xylophone

El ballet	**A. The Ballet**
cortina	**1.** curtain
decoración	**2.** scenery
la bailarina/el bailarín	**3.** dancer
reflector	**4.** spotlight
foro/escenario	**5.** stage
orquesta	**6.** orchestra
podio	**7.** podium
conductor	**8.** conductor
batuta	**9.** baton
músico	**10.** musician
palco	**11.** box seat
luneta	**12.** orchestra seating
entresuelo/mezzanine	**13.** mezzanine
balcón	**14.** balcony
auditorio	**15.** audience
acomodador	**16.** usher
programas	**17.** programs

Comedia musical	**B. Musical Comedy**
coro	**18.** chorus
actor	**19.** actor
actriz	**20.** actress

Grupo (musical) de Rock	**C. Rock Group**
sintetizador	**21.** synthesizer
arreglista	**22.** keyboard player
bajo	**23.** bass guitarist
cantante	**24.** singer
guitarrista principal	**25.** lead guitarist
guitarra eléctrica	**26.** electric guitar
tamborilero/baterista	**27.** drummer

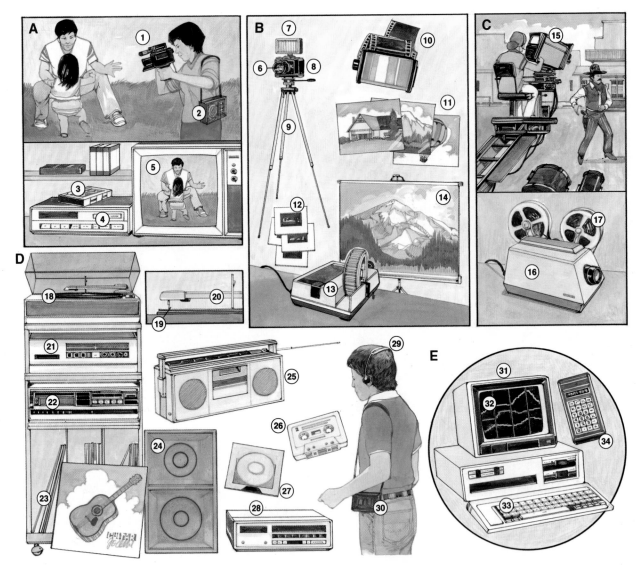

Video	A. Video
cámara de video	1. video camera
mini-cámara	2. Minicam ™
videocassette (cinta)	3. videocassette (tape)
videograbadora	4. VCR (videocassette recorder)
televisor/televisión	5. television

Fotografía	B. Photography
lente	6. lens
flash/destello	7. flash
cámara	8. camera
tripié/trípode	9. tripod
(rollo de) película	10. (roll of) film
fotos/impresiones	11. prints
transparencias	12. slides
proyector de transparencias	13. slide projector
pantalla	14. screen

Película	C. Film
cámara de cine	15. movie camera
proyector	16. projector
(rollo de) película	17. (reel of) film

Audio	D. Audio
tocadiscos/tornamesa	18. turntable
aguja de cartucho	19. cartridge needle
brazo	20. arm
sintonizador/receptor	21. receiver
grabadora	22. cassette deck
discos	23. records
bocina/altoparlante	24. speaker
toca cassettes/cintas	25. stereo cassette player
cassette/cinta	26. cassette
disco compacto	27. compact disc (CD)
tocadiscos compacto	28. compact disc player
audífonos	29. headphones
walkman	30. Sony Walkman

Computadoras	E. Computers
mini-computadora	31. personal computer (PC)
monitor	32. monitor
teclado	33. keyboard
calculadora	34. calculator

Costura	A. Sewing
máquina de coser	**1.** sewing machine
(carrete de) hilo	**2.** (spool of) thread
alfiletero	**3.** pincushion
tela/material/género	**4.** material
tijeras de piquitos	**5.** pinking shears
pieza del patrón	**6.** pattern piece
patrón/modelo	**7.** pattern
ojal	**8.** buttonhole
botón	**9.** button
costura	**10.** seam
dobladillo/ruedo	**11.** hem
bastilla	**12.** hem binding
broche de presión	**13.** snap
presillas	**14.** hook and eye
cinta métrica	**15.** tape measure
cierre	**16.** zipper
(par de) tijeras	**17.** (pair of) scissors

aguja	**18.** needle
puntada	**19.** stitch
alfiler	**20.** pin
dedal	**21.** thimble

Otras actividades de costura	B. Other Needlecrafts
tejido	**22.** knitting
lana	**23.** wool
madeja	**24.** skein
aguja de tejer	**25.** knitting needle
depunto/caneva	**26.** needlepoint
bordado	**27.** embroidery
labor de gancho	**28.** crochet
aguja de gancho	**29.** crochet hook
tejido/tejedora	**30.** weaving
estambre	**31.** yarn
acolchado (sustantivo)	**32.** quilting

en (la ventana)	**1.** at (the window)
sobre/por encima de (el gato negro)	**2.** above (the black cat)
abajo (del gato blanco)	**3.** below (the white cat)
entre (los cojines)	**4.** between (the pillows)
sobre (la alfombra)	**5.** on (the rug)

frente a (la chimenea)	**6.** in front of (the fireplace)
dentro de (el cajón)	**7.** in (the drawer)
debajo de (el escritorio)	**8.** under (the desk)
detrás de (la silla)	**9.** behind (the chair)
sobre (la mesa)	**10.** on top of (the table)
junto a (la TV)	**11.** next to (the TV)

a través de (el faro)	**1.** through (the lighthouse)
alrededor de (el faro)	**2.** around (the lighthouse)
hacia abajo de (la colina)	**3.** down (the hill)
hacia (el hoyo)	**4.** toward (the hole)
lejos de (el hoyo)	**5.** away from (the hole)
al otro lado de (el agua)	**6.** across (the water)

fuera de (el agua)	**7.** out of (the water)
sobre (el puente)	**8.** over (the bridge)
a/hacia (la cancha de golf)	**9.** to (the course)
de/desde (la cancha de golf)	**10.** from (the course)
a/hacia arriba de (la colina)	**11.** up (the hill)
hacia dentro de (el hoyo)	**12.** into (the hole)

Días de la semana / Days of the Week

Días de la semana	Days of the Week
domingo	Sunday
lunes	Monday
martes	Tuesday
miércoles	Wednesday
jueves	Thursday
viernes	Friday
sábado	Saturday

Meses del año / Months of the Year

Meses del año	Months of the Year
enero	January
febrero	February
marzo	March
abril	April
mayo	May
junio	June
julio	July
agosto	August
septiembre	September
octubre	October
noviembre	November
diciembre	December

Números / Numbers

Números		Numbers
cero	0	zero
uno	1	one
dos	2	two
tres	3	three
cuatro	4	four
cinco	5	five
seis	6	six
siete	7	seven
ocho	8	eight
nueve	9	nine
diez	10	ten
once	11	eleven
doce	12	twelve
trece	13	thirteen
catorce	14	fourteen
quince	15	fifteen
dieciséis	16	sixteen
diecisiete	17	seventeen
dieciocho	18	eighteen
diecinueve	19	nineteen
veinte	20	twenty
veintiuno	21	twenty-one
treinta	30	thirty
cuarenta	40	forty
cincuenta	50	fifty
sesenta	60	sixty
setenta	70	seventy
ochenta	80	eighty
noventa	90	ninety
cien/un ciento	100	a/one hundred
quinientos	500	five hundred
seiscientos veintiuno	621	six hundred (and) twenty-one
mil/un mil	1,000	a/one thousand
un millón	1,000,000	a/one million

Colors / Colores

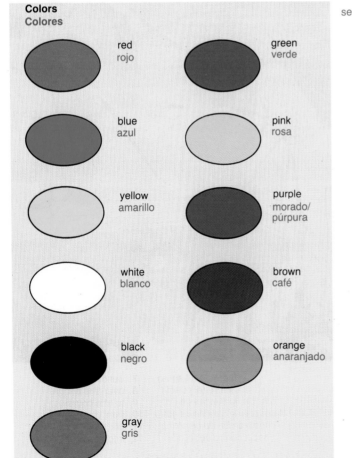

red / rojo	green / verde
blue / azul	pink / rosa
yellow / amarillo	purple / morado/púrpura
white / blanco	brown / café
black / negro	orange / anaranjado
gray / gris	

Two numbers occur after words in the index: the first refers to the page where the word is illustrated and the second to the item number of the word on that page. For example, above [ə bŭv**/**] **102** 2 means that the word *above* is the item numbered 2 on page 102. If only a bold number appears, then that word is part of the unit title or a subtitle.

The index includes a pronunciation guide for all the words illustrated in the book. This guide uses symbols commonly found in dictionaries for native speakers. These symbols, unlike those used in transcription systems such as the International Phonetic Alphabet, tend to preserve spelling and so should help you to become more aware of the connections between written English and spoken English.

Consonants

[b] as in **back** [băk]   [k] as in **kite** [kīt]   [sh] as in **shell** [shĕl]
[ch] as in **cheek** [chēk]   [l] as in **leaf** [lēf]   [t] as in **tape** [tāp]
[d] as in **date** [dāt]   [m] as in **man** [măn]   [th] as in **three** [thrē]
[dh] as in **the** [dh]   [n] as in **neck** [nĕk]   [v] as in **vine** [vīn]
[f] as in **face** [fās]   [ng] as·in **ring** [rĭng]   [w] as in **waist** [wāst]
[g] as in **gas** [găs]   [p] as in **pack** [păk]   [y] as in **yam** [yăm]
[h] as in **half** [hăf]   [r] as in **rake** [rāk]   [z] as in **zoo** [zo͞o]
[j] as in **jack** [jăk]   [s] as in **sand** [sănd]   [zh] as in **measure** [mĕzh**/**ər]

Vowels

[ā] as in **bake** [bāk]   [ī] as in **lime** [līm]   [o͞o] as in **cool** [ko͞ol]
[ă] as in **back** [băk]   [ĭ] as in **lip** [lĭp]   [o͝o] as in **book** [bo͝ok]
[ä] as in **bar** [bär]   [ï] as in **beer** [bïr]   [ow] as in **cow** [kow]
[ē] as in **beat** [bēt]   [ō] as in **post** [pōst]   [oy] as in **boy** [boy]
[ĕ] as. in **bed** [bĕd]   [ŏ] as in **box** [bŏks]   [ŭ] as in **cut** [kŭt]
[ë] as in **bear** [bër]   [ö] as in **claw** [klö]   [ü] as in **curb** [kürb]
                                   or **for** [för]   [ə] as in **above** [ə bŭv**/**]

All pronunciation symbols used are alphabetical except for the schwa [ə], which is the most frequent vowel sound in English. If you use it appropriately in unstressed syllables, your pronunciation will sound more natural.

You should note that an umlaut ([¨]) calls attention to the special quality of vowels before [r]. (The sound [ö] can also represent a vowel not followed by [r] as in *claw*.) You should listen carefully to native speakers to discover how these vowels actually sound.

Stress

This guide also follows the system for marking stress used in many dictionaries for native speakers.
    (1) Stress is not marked if a word consisting of a single syllable occurs in isolation.
    (2) Where stress is marked, two levels are distinguished:
        a bold accent [**/**] is placed after each syllable with primary stress,
        a light accent [/] is placed after each syllable with secondary stress.

Syllable Boundaries

Syllable boundaries are indicated by a single space.

NOTE: The pronunciation used in this index is based on patterns of American English. There has been no attempt to represent all of the varieties of American English. Students should listen to native speakers to hear how the language actually sounds in a particular region.

above [ə bŭv/] **102** 2

abdomen [ăb/də mən] **4** 14

accelerator [ăk sĕl/ə rā/tər] **50** 27

accordion [ə kör/dē ən] **98** 28

accountant [ə kown/tənt] **86** 18

acorn [ā/körn] **61** 33b

acorn squash [ā/körn skwŏsh/] **7** 28

across [ə krös/] **103** 6

actor [ăk/tər] **99** 19

actress [ăk/trəs] **99** 20

acute angle [ə kyōōt/ăng/gəl] **79** 8

address [ă/drĕs] **46** 11

adjectives [ăj/ĭk tĭvz] **24, 25**

aerial tramway [ër/ē əl trăm/wā] **55** 31

Africa [ă/frĭ kə] **70** 4

after-shave lotion [ăf/tər shāv lō/shən] **23** 21

ailments [āl/mənts] **40**

air conditioner [ër/kən dĭ/shə nər] **32** 11

air filter [ër/fĭl/tər] **51** 52

Air Force [ër/förs/] **48** 19

air mattress [ër/mă/trəs] **91** 26

air pump [ër/pŭmp/] **53** 13

air travel [ër/tră/vəl] **56**

aircraft [ër/krăft/] **57**

aircraft carrier [ër/krăft kăr/yər] **48** 4

aircraft types [ër/krăft tīps/] **57**

(airmail) envelope [ër/māl ĕn/və lōp] **46** 16

airman [ër/mən] **48** 20

airport check-in [ër/pört chĕk/ĭn] **56**

aisle [ī/əl] **14** 10, **56** 23

Alabama [ăl/ə bă/mə] **72** 1

alarm clock [ə lärm/klŏk] **32** 8

Alaska [ə lăs/kə] **72** 2

alcohol [ăl/kə höl/] **39** 22

alligator [ăl/ə gā/tər] **65** 8

almond(s) [ö/mənd(z)] **9** 31

Alps [ălps] **70** 44

Amazon River [ă/mə zŏn rĭv/ər] **71** 59

ambulance [ăm/byə ləns] **42** 6

amphibians [ăm fĭ/bē ənz] **65**

ammunition [ăm/yə nĭsh/ən] **48**

anchor [ăng/kər] **58** 24

Andes [ăn/dēz] **71** 43

ankle [ăng/kəl] **5** 49

animals [ăn/ə məlz] **62-69**

ant [ănt] **63** 12

Antarctic Ocean [ănt ärk/tĭk ō/shən] **70** 14

Antarctica [ănt ärk/tĭ kə] **70** 7

anteater [ănt/ē/tər] **66** 5

antenna [ăn tĕn/ə] **51** 46, **62** 1b

antler [ănt/lər] **67** 35a

apartment house [ə pärt/mənt hows/] **45** 23

apex [ā/pĕks] **79** 21

Appalachian Mountains [ăp/ə lā/chē ən mown/tənz] **71** 41

apple [ă/pəl] **8** 2

apricot [ăp/rə kŏt/] **9** 25

apron [ā/prən] **16** 6

aquatic mammals [ə kwŏ/tĭk mă/məlz] **68**

Arabian Sea [ə rā/bē ən sē/] **70** 30

arc [ärk] **79** 16

architect [är/kə tĕkt/] **86** 8

Arctic [ärk/tĭk] **70** 8

Arizona [ăr/ə zō/nə] **72** 3

Arkansas [är/kən sö/] **72** 4

arm [ärm] **4** 6, **100** 20

armadillo [är/mə dĭl/ō] **66** 2

armed forces [ärmd/för/səz] **48**

armpit [ärm/pĭt/] **4** 10

armrest [ärm/rĕst/] **50** 3

Army [är/mē] **48** 15

around [ə rownd/] **103** 2

artery [är/tə rē] **5** 69

artichoke [är/tə chōk/] **6** 11

artist [är/təst] **86** 3

arts [ärts] **86**

ashtray [ăsh/trā/] **16** 29

Asia [ā/zhə] **70** 5

asparagus [ə spăr/ə gəs] **6** 18

asteroid [ăs/tə royd/] **74** 20

astronaut [ăs/trə nöt/] **75** 5

at [ăt] **102** 1

Atacama Desert [ăt/ə kŏ/mə dĕz/ərt] **71** 50

athletic supporter [ăth lĕ/tĭk sə pör/tər] **22** 4

atlas [ăt/ləs] **47** 20

attachments [ə tăch/mənts] **35** 17

attendant [ə tĕn/dənt] **39** 8, **53** 12

audience [ö/dē əns] **99** 15

audio [ö/dē ō/] **100**

aunt [ănt] **3** 6

Australia [ö strāl/yə] **70** 6

author [ö/thər] **47** 8

automatic transmission [ö/tə măt/ĭk trănz mĭ/shən] **50**

avocado [ăv/ə kŏ/dō] **9** 33

away from [ə wā/frŭm] **103** 5

axe [ăks] **42** 14

baboon [bă bōōn/] **69** 19

baby [bā/bē] **2** 5

baby carriage [bā/bē kăr/ĭj] **45** 27

baby lotion [bā/bē lō/shən] **33** 6

baby powder [bā/bē pow/dər] **33** 7

baby wipes [bā/bē wīps/] **33** 8

baby's room [bā/bēz rōōm/] **33**

back [băk] **4** 11, **23** 19

backache [băk/āk/] **40** 8

backboard [băk/börd/] **92** 19

backhoe [băk/hō/] **82** 26

backpack [băk/păk/] **19** 4

backseat [băk/sēt/] **50** 32

backyard [băk/yärd/] **27**

back-up light [băk/əp līt/] **50** 30

bacon [bā/kən] **10** 11, **18, 33**

badge [băj] **43** 5

Baffin Bay [băf/ən bā/] **70** 16

bag [băg] **12** 8, **15** 25, **21** 35

baggage [băg/ĭj] **56** 8

bake [bāk] **31** 14

baked beans [bākt/bēnz/] **18** 3

baked goods [bākt gōōdz/] **14** 11

baked potato [bākt/pə tā/tō] **18** 20

baker [bā/kər] **84** 8

bakery [bā/kə rē] **44** 6

balance beam [băl/əns bēm/] **94** 24

balcony [băl/kə nē] **99** 14

(bale of) hay [bāl/əv hā/] **81** 13

ball [böl] **5** 52

ballet [bă lā/] **99**

ballfields [böl/fēldz/] **93**

ballpoint pen [böl/poynt pĕn/] **76** 22

Baltic Sea [böl/tĭk sē/] **70** 22

bananas [bə nă/nəz] **9** 20

Band-Aid [bănd/ād/] **39** 4

band shell [bănd/shĕl/] **87** 2

bandage [băn/dĭj] **39** 24

anister [băn/ə stər] **28** 11

anjo [băn/jō/] **98** 5

anking [băng/kĭng] **86**

ar [bär] **13** 18, **16** 24

ar stool [bär/stool/] **16** 25

arber [bär/bər] **84** 3

arents Sea [băr/ənts sē/] **70** 23

arge [bärj] **58** 12

ark [bärk] **61** 35c

arn [bärn] **81** 5

arnyard [bärn/yärd/] **81** 8

arrel [băr/əl] **48** 23

arricade [băr/ə kād/] **82** 21

artender [bär/těn/dər] **16** 21

ase [bās] **79** 7, **93** 6

aseball [bās/böl/] **92**

aseball diamond [bās/böl dī/mənd] **93**

aseline [bās/līn/] **95** 4

asin [bā/sən] **39** 16

asket [băs/kət] **92** 20

asketball [băs/kət böl/] **92**, **92** 21

ass [bās] **98** 10

ass guitarist [bās/gə tär/əst] **99** 23

assoon [bă soon/] **98** 14

at [băt] **66** 4, **92** 5

atboy [băt/boy/] **93** 18

ath mat [băth/ măt/] **34** 12

ath towel [băth/ tow/əl] **34** 24

athing suit [bā/dhĭng soot/] **90** 18

athing trunks [bā/ dhĭng trŭngks/] **91** 33

athrobe [băth/ rōb] **22** 20

athroom [băth/ room/] **34**

athtub [băth/ tŭb/] **34** 11

aton [bə tŏn/] **99** 9

atter [băt/ ər] **92** 7, **93** 14

attery [băt/ ə rē] **51** 54

atting helmet [băt/ĭng hěl/mət] **92** 6

attleship [băt/ əl shĭp/] **48** 5

ay of Bengal [bā/ əv běn göl/] **70** 32

ayonet [bā/ ə nět/] **48** 24

ays [bāz] **70**

ach [bēch] **90**

ach ball [bēch/ böl/] **90** 11

ach chair [bēch/ chěr/] **90** 20

ach towel [bēch/ tow/ əl] **90** 15

beach umbrella [bēch/ əm brěl/ ə] **90** 21

beads [bēdz] **23** 7

beak [bēk] **64** 3a

beaker [bē/ kər] **78** 23

beard [bĭrd] **4** 39

bears [bërz] **69**

beat [bēt] **31** 8

Beaufort Sea [bō/ fərt sē/] **70** 15

beaver [bē/vər] **66** 12

bed [běd] **32** 21

bed rest [běd/ rěst/] **41** 1

bedroom [běd/room/] **32**

bedspread [běd/sprěd/] **32** 23

bee [bē] **63** 19

beef [bēf] **10** 1

beef stew [bēf/ stoo/] **18** 14

beer [bïr] **16** 23

beet(s) [bēts] **7** 33

beetle [bē/təl] **63** 10

behind [bə hīnd/] **102** 9

below [bə lō/] **102** 3

belt [bělt] **20** 16

bench [běnch] **43** 16, **44** 14, **78** 24, **87** 10

beret [bə rā/] **19** 22

Bering Sea [běr/ĭng sē/] **70** 34

berries [běr/ēz] **8**

between [bə twēn/] **102** 4

beverages [běv/rə jəz] **14** 14

bib [bĭb] **33** 20

bicycle [bī/sĭ kəl] **52** 15

big [bĭg] **24** 8

(Big Dipper) constellation [bĭg/ dĭ/pər kŏn stə lā/shən] **74** 3

big toe [bĭg/ tō/] **5** 53

bike stand [bīk/ stănd/] **52** 14

biker [bī/kər] **90** 4

bikes [bīks] **52**

(bikini) panties [bə kē/ nē păn/ tēz] **22** 11

bill [bĭl] **64** 24a

bin [bĭn] **15** 16

binding [bīn/ dĭng] **95** 16

binoculars [bə nŏk/ yə lərs] **90** 7

birch [bürch] **61** 32

birds [bürdz] **64**

biscuit [bĭs/ kət] **18** 27

bison [bī/sən] **67** 19

bit [bĭt] **37** 43a

black bear [blăk/ bër/] **69** 21

black bean(s) [blăk/ bēn(z)/] **6** 14

black eye [blăk/ ī/] **40** 5

Black Sea [blăk/ sē/] **70** 26

blackberries [blăk/ bër/ ēz] **8** 12

bladder [blă/ dər] **5** 72

blade [blād] **94** 27

blanket [blăng/ket] **32** 20

blazer [blā/ zer] **20** 2

bleach [blēch] **35** 26

blender [blěn/ dər] **30** 12

blimp [blĭmp] **57** 5

blinds [blīndz] **32** 12

block [blŏk] **33** 32

blouse [blows] **21** 34

blue jay [bloo/ ja/] **64** 8

(blue) jeans [bloo/ jēnz/] **19** 6

blueberries [bloo/bër/ēz] **8** 14

blueprints [bloo/prĭnts/] **82** 6

blush [blŭsh] **23** 32

board [börd] **82** 16

boarding [bör/dĭng] **56**

boarding pass [bör/dĭng păs/] **56** 18

boardwalk [börd/wök/] **90** 1

body [bŏ/dē] **4**

boil [boyl] **31** 16

bollard [bŏl/ ərd] **58** 26

bolt [bōlt] **37** 38

bomb [bŏm] **48** 3

bomber [bŏm/ ər] **48** 2

bongos [bŏng/ gōz] **98** 22

book [book] **13** 17

(book of) matches [book/ əv mă/ chəz] **16** 28

bookcase [book/ kās] **28** 22, **83** 20

bookstore [book/ stör] **45** 18

boom [boom] **59** 7

booth [booth] **16** 9

boots [boots] **19** 21, **21** 32

bottle [bŏt/ əl] **12** 3, **33** 17

bottle opener [bŏt/ əl ō/ pə nər] **30** 6

bounce [bowns] **97** 11

bow [bō] **98** 7a

bow [bow] **58** 5

bowl [bōl] **13** 23

bowling [bōl/ĭng] **94**

bowling ball [bōl′ĭng böl′] **94** 6

box [bŏks] **13** 12

box seat [bŏks′ sēt′] **99** 11

box spring [bŏks′ sprĭng′] **32** 18

boxer shorts [bŏk′ sər shörts′] **22** 2

boxing [bŏk′ sĭng] **94**

boy's frame [boyz′ frām′] **52** 11

bra(ssiere) [brŏ]/[brə zïr′] **22** 13

brace [brās] **36** 9

bracelet [brās′lət] **23** 9

brain [brān] **5** 57

brake [brāk] **50** 26, **52** 17

brake light [brāk′ līt′] **50** 29

branch [brănch] **61** 35a

brass [brăs] **98**

bread [brĕd] **14** 12

bread and butter plate
  [brĕd′ ənd bŭt′ ər plāt′] **29** 11

break [brāk] **31** 7

breast [brĕst] **11** 21

bricks [brĭks] **82** 12

bridle path [brīd′ əl păth′] **87** 7

briefcase [brēf′ kās′] **21** 37

briefs [brēfs] **22** 12

broccoli [brŏk′ ə lē] **6** 2

broil [broyl] **31** 13

broiler [broy′ lər] **30** 33

broken bone [brō′ kən bōn′] **40** 15

broom [brōōm] **35** 7

brother [brŭdh′ ər] **3** 9

brother-in-law [brŭdh′ ər ən lö′] **3** 11

bruise [brōōz] **40** 17

brush [brŭsh] **76** 18

brussels sprouts [brŭs′ əl sprowts′] **6** 4

bucket [bŭk′ ət] **35** 15

bucket seat [bŭk′ ət sēt′] **50** 16

buckle [bŭk′ əl] **20** 17

bud [bŭd] **60** 18a

buffet [bə fā′] **29** 29

builder [bĭl′ dər] **82** 5

building number [bĭl′ dĭng nŭm′ bər]
  45 24

bulb [bŭlb] **60** 8a

bull [bŏŏl] **67** 34

bulldozer [bŏŏl′ dō′ zər] **82** 27

bullet [bŏŏl′ ĭt] **48** 26

bulletin board [bŏŏl′ ĭ tən börd′] **76** 7

bumper [bŭm′ pər] **33** 5

bun [bŭn] **18** 7

bunch [bŭnch] **8** 1

Bunsen burner [bŭn′ sən bür′ nər]
  78 20

buoy [bōō′ ē]/[boy] **58** 16

bureau [byŏŏr′ ō] **32** 9

burn [bürn] **17** 14, **40** 18

burner [bür′ nər] **30** 29

bus [bŭs] **53** 20, **54**

bus driver [bŭs′ drī′ vər] **54** 3

bus stop [bŭs′ stŏp′] **44** 13

busboy [bŭs′ boy′] **16** 3

bushes [bŏŏsh′ əz] **61** 41

business workers [biz′ nəs wür′ kərz] **86**

butcher [bŏŏ′ chər] **84** 13

butter [bŭt′ ər] **18** 18

buttercup [bŭt′ ər kŭp′] **60** 17

butterfly [bŭt′ ər flī′] **63** 3

buttocks [bŭt′ əks] **4** 15

button [bŭt′ ən] **20** 3, **101** 9

buttonhole [bŭt′ ən hōl′] **101** 8

C-clamp [sē′ klămp′] **36** 2

cab driver [kăb′ drī′ vər] **55** 26

cabbage [kăb′ ĭj] **6** 3

cabin [kăb′ ĭn] **56** 19

cabin cruiser [kăb′ ĭn krōō′ zər] **59** 16

cabinet [kăb′ ə nət] **30** 22

cable [kā′ bəl] **52** 23

cable car [kā′ bəl kär′] **55** 32

cactus [kăk′ təs] **61** 40

calculator [kăl′ kyə lā′ tər] **83** 19,
  100 34

calendar [căl′ ən dər] **83** 9

calf [kăf] **4** 20, **67** 31

California [kăl′ ə för′ nyə] **72** 5

call card [köl′ kärd′] **47** 6

call number [köl′ nŭm′ bər] **47** 7

call slip [köl′ slĭp′] **47** 12

camel [kăm′ əl] **67** 33

camera [kăm′ ər ə] **100** 8

cameraperson [kăm′ ər ə pür′ sən] **86** 10

camisole [kăm′ ə sōl′] **22** 9

camp stove [kămp′ stōv′] **89** 25

camper [kăm′ pər] **53** 16

campfire [kămp′ fīr′] **89** 31

camping [kăm′ pĭng] **89**

can [kăn] **12** 10

can opener [kăn′ ō′ pə nər] **30** 4

canary [kə nër′ ē] **64** 14

candle [kăn′ dəl] **29** 27

candlestick [kăn′ dəl stĭk′] **29** 28

canister [kăn′ ə stər] **30** 15

canned goods [kănd′ gŏŏdz′] **14** 13

cannon [kăn′ ən] **48** 11

canoe [kə nōō′] **59** 2

cantaloupe [kăn′ tə lōp′] **9** 36

canyon [kăn′ yən] **88** 3

cap [kăp] **19** 2, **21** 43, **92** 11

capsule [kăp′ səl] **41** 5

car [kär] **54** 9

card catalog [kärd′ kăt′ ə lög] **47** 4

cardigan [kär′ dĭ gən] **21** 26

cardinal [kärd′ nəl] **64** 11

cargo [kär′ gō] **58** 10

cargo area [kär′ gō ër′ ē ə] **57** 12

cargo bay [kär′ gō bā′] **75** 9

cargo door [kär′ gō dör′] **57** 13

Caribbean Sea [kăr′ ə bē′ ən sē′]
  70 20

carpenter [kär′ pən tər] **85** 2

carpenter's rule [kär′ pən tərz rōōl′]
  36 1

carrot(s) [kăr′ ət(s)] **7** 32

carry [kăr′ ē] **26** 16

carry-on bag [kăr′ ē ŏn băg′] **56** 2

cars [kärz] **50-51**

carton [kär′ tən] **12** 1

cartridge needle [kär′ trĭj nē′ dəl]
  100 19

carve [kärv] **31** 6

cash register [kăsh′ rĕ′ jə stər] **15** 21

cashew(s) [kăsh′ ōō(z)] **9** 27

cashier [kă shïr′] **15** 22

Caspian Sea [kăs′ pē ən sē′] **70** 27

casserole dish [kăs′ ə rōl dĭsh′] **30** 1·

cassette [kə sĕt′] **100** 26

cassette deck [kə sĕt′ dĕk′] **100** 22

cast [kăst] **39** 5

cat [kăt] **68** 4

catch [kăch] **96** 4

catcher [kăch′ ər] **92** 2, **93** 16

catcher's mask [kăch′ ərz măsk′] **92** 3

catcher's mitt [kăch′ ərz mĭt′] **92** 4

caterpillar [kăt′ ər pĭl′ ər] **63** 1

cattle [kăt′ əl] **81** 20

Caucasus [kö′ kə səs] **71** 45

cauliflower [kôl′ ə flow′ ər] **6** 1

ceiling [sē′ lĭng] **28** 2

ceiling fan [sē′ lĭng făn′] **28** 1

celery [sĕl′ ə rē] **6** 10

cello [chĕl′ o] **98** 9

cement [sə mĕnt′] **82** 10

cement mixer [sə mĕnt′ mĭk′ sər] **82** 25

cement truck [sə mĕnt′ trŭk′] **49** 13

center [sĕn′ tər] **79** 13, **93** 27

center divider [sĕn′ tər də vī′ dər] **53** 18, **82** 24

center fielder [sĕn′ tər fēl′ dər] **93** 2

center lane [sĕn′ tər lān′] **53** 6

centerboard [sĕn′ tər börd′] **59** 6

centipede [sĕn′ tə pēd′] **63** 22

chain [chān] **23** 5, **52** 18

chair [chër] **29** 17

chalk [chök] **76** 10

chalk tray [chök′ trā′] **76** 9

chalkboard [chök′ börd′] **76** 5

chandelier [shăn′ də lĭr′] **29** 3

change (the sheets) [chānj′ dhə shēts′] **38** 13

changing table [chān′ jĭng tā′ bəl] **33** 9

charcoal briquettes [chär′ kōl brĭ kĕts′] **27** 23

chart [chärt] **39** 10

check [chĕk] **15** 27, **16** 14

checked [chĕkt] **24** 18

checkout counter [chĕk′ owt kown′ tər] **15** 26

checkout desk [chĕk′ owt dĕsk′] **47** 2

cheerleaders [chĭr′ lē′ dərz] **93** 20

cheek [chēk] **4** 35

cherries [chër′ ēz] **9** 19

cherry picker [chër′ ē pĭk′ ər] **82** 18

chest [chĕst] **4** 12

chest of drawers [chĕst′ əv drörz′] **32** 30

chestnut(s) [chĕs′ nŭt(s)] **9** 32

chick [chĭk] **64** 22

chicken [chĭk′ ən] **11** 24, **64** 23

child's seat [chīldz′ sēt′] **50** 33

children [chĭl′ drən] **2** 7

chills [chĭlz] **40** 4

chimney [chĭm′ nē] **27** 9

chimpanzee [chĭm păn′ zē] **69** 16

chin [chĭn] **4** 3

china [chī′ nə] **29** 1

china closet [chī′ nə klŏz′ ət] **29** 2

chipmunk [chĭp′ mŭnk] **66** 6

chop [chŏp] **26** 11, **31** 11

chops [chŏps] **10** 9, **10** 15

chorus [kör′ əs] **99** 18

(chrysanthe)mum [krə săn′ thə məm]/[mŭm] **60** 4

cigarette [sĭg′ ə rĕt′] **16** 31

circle [sür′ kəl] **79** 11

circuit breaker [sür′ kət brā′ kər] **35** 5

circular saw [sür′ kyə lər sö′] **36** 20

circumference [sür kŭm′ fə rəns] **79** 17

citrus fruits [sĭ′ trəs frōōts′] **8**

city [sĭt′ ē] **44-45**

clam(s) [klăm(z)] **11** 32

clamp [klămp] **78** 7

clarinet [klăr′ ə nĕt′] **98** 16

clasp [klăsp] **23** 17

classroom [klăs′ rōōm′] **76**

claw [klö] **62** 13a, **68** 2a

clean [klēn] **24** 6, **26** 2

cleanser [klĕn′ zər] **35** 9

clear [klĭr] **17** 6

cliff [klĭf] **89** 21

clip-on earring [klĭp′ ŏn ĭr′ ĭng] **23** 15

clock [klŏk] **76** 2

close (v) [klōz] **77** 5

closed [klōzd] **24** 16

closet [klŏz′ ət] **32** 3

cloth diaper [klöth′ dī′ pər] **33** 13

clothes [klōz] **19-24**

clothesline [klōz′ līn′] **35** 19

clothespins [klōz′ pĭnz′] **35** 20

cloudy [klow′ dē] **25** 2

clove [klōv] **7** 25a

cloverleaf [klō′ vər lēf′] **53** 4

clubs [klŭbz] **95** 5

clutch [klŭch] **50** 25

coach [kōch] **93** 21

coal [kōl] **80** 7

coal mine [kōl′ mīn′] **80** 6

coaster [kō′ stər] **16** 27

coat [kōt] **19** 24, **42** 13

cob [kŏb] **6** 12a

cobra [kō′ brə] **65** 11

cockpit [kŏk′ pĭt′] **56** 13

cockroach [kŏk′ rōch′] **63** 9

cocktail lounge [kŏk′ tāl lownj′] **16**

cocktail waitress [kŏk′ tāl wā′ trəs] **16** 32

cocoon [kə kōōn′] **63** 2

coconut [kō′ kə nŭt′] **8** 3

coffee [kö′ fē] **18** 35

coffeemaker [kö′ fē mā′ kər] **30** 31

coffeepot [kö′ fē pŏt′] **29** 18

coffee table [kö′ fē tā′ bəl] **28** 26

coins [koynz] **13** 26

colander [kŏl′ ən dər] **30** 7

cold [kōld] **25** 10, **40** 11

cold water faucet [kōld′ wŏ tər fö′ sət] **34** 18

collar [kŏl′ ər] **20** 20

colonial-style house [kə lō′ nē əl stīl hows′] **27**

Colorado [kŏl′ ə rŏd′ ō] **72** 6

column [kŏl′ əm] **50** 13

comb [kōm] **32** 6

combine (n) [kŏm′ bīn] **81** 17

comet [kŏm′ ət] **74** 2

comforter [kŭm′ fər tər] **32** 22

command module [kə mănd′ mŏj′ ōōl] **75** 8

communication satellite [kə myōō′ nə kā shən săt′ ə līt] **75** 2

commuter [kə myōō′ tər] **55** 17

commuter train [kə myōō′ tər trān′] **55** 14

compact disc (CD) [kŏm′ păkt dĭsk′]/[sē′ dē′] **100** 27

compact disc player [kŏm′ păkt dĭsk′ plā′ ər] **100** 28

computer [kəm pyōō′ tər] **76** 8, **83** 16, **100**

computer programmer [kəm pyōō′ tər prō′ grăm ər] **86** 16

conductor [kən dŭk′ tər] **54** 7, **99** 8

cone [kōn] **61** 34b, **79** 28, **82** 19

conga [kŏng′ gə] **98** 20

Congo River [kŏng′ gō rĭv′ ər] **71** 62

Connecticut [kə nĕ′ tĭ kət] **72** 7

constellation [kŏn′ stə lā′ shən] **74** 3

construction [kən strŭk′ shən] **82**

(construction) boots [kən strŭk′ shən bōōts′] **21** 32

construction site [kən strŭk′ shən sīt′] **82**

construction worker
[kən strŭk′ shən wür′ kər] **82** 14

container [kən tā′ nər] **12** 2, **58** 7

(container)ship [kən tā′ nər shĭp′] **58** 9

containers [kən tā′ nərz] **12**

continents [kŏn′ tə nənts] **70**

control tower [kən trōl′ tow′ər] **57** 20

conveyor belt [kən vā′ər bĕlt] **15** 23,
56 12

cook (n) [kŏŏk] **16** 1

cook (v) [kŏŏk] **17** 4

cookie [kŏŏk′ ē] **18** 22

cool [kŏŏl] **25** 9

cooler [kŏŏ′ lər] **91** 41

cooling tower [kŏŏ′ lĭng tow′ər] **80** 16

copilot [kō′ pī lət] **56** 16

cord [körd] **32** 26a, **54** 1

(corduroy) pants [kör′ də roy pănts′]
21 27

core [kör] **8** 2b, **80** 14

cork [körk] **16** 18

corkscrew [körk′ skrŏŏ′] **16** 17

corn [körn] **6** 12, **60** 24

corner [kör′ nər] **44** 3

corral [kə răl′] **81** 24

cosmetics [kŏz mĕt′ ĭks] **23**

cotton balls [kŏt′ ən bölz′] **39** 23

cotton swab [kŏt′ ən swŏb′] **33** 10

counter [kown′ tər] **30** 27

court [kört] **43**, **94** 13

court officer [kört ö′ fə sər] **43** 19

court reporter [kört′ rə pör′ tər] **43** 14

cousin [kŭz′ ən] **3** 7

cow [kow] **67** 32

cowboy [kow′ boy′] **81** 21

cowgirl [kow′ gürl′] **81** 22

crab(s) [kră b(z)] **11** 36, **62** 9

cradle [krā′ dəl] **33** 26

cranberries [krăn′ bĕr′ ēz] **8** 13

crane [krān] **58** 6

creamer [krē′ mər] **29** 24

crew [krŏŏ] **75** 12

(crewneck) sweater
[krŏŏ′ nĕk swĕt′ ər] **19** 7

crib [krĭb] **33** 4

criket [krĭk′ ət] **63** 5

crime [krīm] **43**

crochet [krō shā′] **101** 28

crochet hook [krō′ shā′ hŏŏk′] **101** 29

crocus [krō′ kəs] **60** 9

cross-country skiing
[krös′ kŭn trē skē′ ĭng] **94**

crosswalk [krös′ wök′] **44** 4

crow [krō] **64** 3

crutch [krŭch] **39** 7

cube [kyŏŏb] **79** 27

cubicle [kyŏŏ′ bə kəl] **83** 5

cucumber(s) [kyŏŏ′ kŭm bər(z)] **7** 20

cuff links [kŭf′ lĭnks′] **23** 12

cup [kŭp] **13** 19, **29** 20

curb [kürb] **45** 26

curtain [kür′ tən] **32** 10, **99** 1

curtain rings [kür′ tən rĭngz′] **34** 2

curtain rod [kür′ tən röd′] **34** 1

curve [kürv] **79** 3

cushion [kŏŏsh′ ən] **28** 24

customer [kŭs′ tə mər] **15** 17

cut (v) [kŭt] **31** 9

cut (n) [kŭt] **40** 16

cutting board [kŭt′ ĭng börd′] **30** 26

cylinder [sĭl′ ĭn dər] **79** 26

cymbals [sĭm′ bəlz] **98** 18

daffodil [dăf′ ə dĭl] **60** 8

dairy cow [dër′ ē kow′] **81** 11

dairy farm [dër′ ē färm′] **81**

dairy products [dër′ ē prŏd′ ŭkts] **14** 4

daisy [dā′ zē] **60** 5

dam [dăm] **80** 18

dance [dăns] **99**

dancer [dăn′ sər] **99** 3

dark [därk] **24** 10

dashboard [dăsh′ börd′] **50** 19

date [dāt] **9** 23

daughter [dö′ tər] **3** 15

deck [dĕk] **27** 5, **58** 22

deer [dïr] **67** 26

defendant [də fĕn′ dənt] **43** 23

defense attorney [də fĕns′ ə tür′ nē]
43 22

Delaware [dĕl′ ə wär′] **72** 8

deli counter [dĕl′ ē kown′ tər] **14** 1

delivery boy [də lĭv′ ə rē boy′] **85** 10

delivery person [də lĭv′ ə rē pür′ sən]
49 10

dental care [dĕn′ təl kër′] **39**

dentist [dĕn′ tĭst] **39** 17

department store [də pärt′ mənt stör′]
44 5

depth [dĕpth] **79** 33

derrick [dĕr′ ĭk] **80** 2

deserts [dĕz′ ərts] **71**

desk [dĕsk] **28** 14, **76** 16, **83** 13

detective [də tĕk′ tĭv] **43** 2

diagonal [dī ăg′ ə nəl] **79** 20

diameter [dī ăm′ ə tər] **79** 12

dictionary [dĭk′ shə nër′ ē] **47** 24

diesel fuel [dē′ zəl fyŏŏ′ əl] **80** 34

dig [dĭg] **26** 3

dime [dīm] **13** 29

dinghy [dĭng′ ē] **59** 18

dining room [dī′ nĭng rŏŏm′] **29**

dipstick [dĭp′ stĭk′] **51** 58

dirt bike [dürt′ bīk′] **52** 8

disc jockey (DJ) [dĭsk′ jŏk′ ē]/[dē′ jā]
86 9

dirty [dür′ tē] **24** 5

dish drainer [dĭsh′ drā′ nər] **30** 2

dish towel [dĭsh′ tow′ əl] **30** 18

dishwasher [dĭsh′ wŏsh′ ər] **30** 1

dishwashing liquid
[dĭsh′ wŏsh ĭng lĭ′ kwĭd] **30** 10

disposable diaper
[dĭs pō′ zə bəl dī′ pər] **33** 12

dissection kit [dĭ sĕk′ shən kĭt′] **78** 33

dive [dīv] **97** 14

dock [dŏk] **58** 28

doctor [dŏk′ tər] **39** 11

dogs [dögz] **69**

dogwood [dög′ wŏŏd′] **61** 28

doll [dŏl] **33** 28

doll house [dŏl′ hows′] **33** 25

dollar bills [dŏl′ ər bĭlz′] **13** 25

dolly [dŏl′ ē] **56** 6

dolphin [dŏl′ fĭn] **68** 13

donkey [dŏng′ kē] **67** 23

door handle [dör′ hăn′ dəl] **50** 4

door lock [dör′ lŏk′] **50** 1

doorman [dör′ mən] **85** 11

down [down] **103** 3

down vest [down′ vĕst′] **19** 12

dragonfly [drăg′ ən flī′] **63** 4

drain [drān] **34** 9

drainpipe [drān′ pīp′] **27** 18

drapes [drāps] **28** 23

draw [drö] **77** 11

drawer [drör] **47** 5

dress [drĕs] **20** 22

dried fruits [drīd′ frōōts′] **9**

drill [drĭl] **39** 15

drink [drĭngk] **17** 2

drive [drīv] **97** 15

driveway [drīv′ wā′] **27** 1

drugstore [drŭg′ stör′] **45** 22

drum [drŭm] **98** 19

drummer [drŭm′ ər] **99** 27

drumsticks [drŭm′ stĭks′] **98** 19a

dry [drī] **25** 14, **38** 9

dryer [drī′ər] **35** 24

duck [dŭk] **11** 25, **64** 25

(duck) pond [dŭk′ pŏnd′] **87** 8

dugout [dŭg′ owt′] **93** 13

dump truck [dŭmp′ trŭk′] **49** 14

dust [dŭst] **38** 15

dustpan [dŭst′ păn′] **35** 8

eagle [ē′ gəl] **64** 5

ear [ïr] **4** 34

(ear of) corn [ïr′ əv körn′] **6** 12

earmuffs [ïr′ mŭfs′] **19** 10

earrings [ïr′ ĭngz] **23** 1

Earth [ürth] **74** 8, **13**

east [ēst] **71** 73

East China Sea [ēst′ chī′ nə sē′]
    70 38

eat [ēt] **17** 1

eel [ēl] **65** 4

egg [ĕg] **18** 32, **64** 13

egg roll [ĕg′ rōl′] **18** 25

eggplant [ĕg′ plănt′] **7** 21

elbow [ĕl′ bō] **4** 8

electric drill [ĭ lĕk′ trĭk drĭl′] **37** 43

electric guitar [ĭ lĕk′ trĭk gĭ tär′]
    99 26

electric generator
    [ĭ lĕk′ trĭk gĕn′ ə rā tər] **80** 21

electrical tape [ĭ lĕk′ trĭ kəl tāp′]
    37 34

electrician [ĭ lĕk trĭ′ shən] **85** 6

electricity [ĭ lĕk trĭs′ ĭ tē] **80** 32

electronics [ĭ lĕk trŏn′ ĭks] **100**

elephant [ĕl′ ə fənt] **66** 17

elevator [ĕl′ ə vā′ tər] **45** 17, **80** 9

elm [ĕlm] **61** 36

embroidery [ĕm broi′ də rē] **101** 27

emergency brake [ĭ mür′ jən sē brāk′]
    50 15

emery board [ĕm′ ə rē börd′] **23** 24

encyclopedia [ĕn sī′ klə pē′ dē ə] **47** 25

end table [ĕnd′ tā′ bəl] **28** 29

end zone [ĕnd′ zōn′] **93** 23

energy [ĕn′ ər jē] **80**

engagement ring [ĕn gāj′ mənt rĭng′]
    23 3

engine [ĕn′ jən] **51, 52** 32

engineer [ĕn′ jə nïr′] **55** 15

enter [ĕn′ tər] **77** 14

entrance ramp [ĕn′ trəns rămp′] **53** 21

envelope [ĕn′ və lōp′] **46** 16, **83** 31

equator [ĭ kwā′ tər] **71** 70

erase [ĭ rās′] **77** 3

eraser [ĭ rā′ sər] **76** 11

escarole [ĕs′ kə rōl′] **6** 7

esophagus [ĭ sŏf′ ə gəs] **5** 61

eucalyptus [yōō′ kə lĭp′ təs] **61** 27

Europe [yōōr′ əp] **70** 3

examining table [ĭg zăm′ ə nĭng tā′ bəl]
    39 6

exhaust pipe [ĭg zöst′ pīp′] **52** 33

exit ramp [ĕg′ zĭt rămp′] **53** 2

exit sign [ĕg′ zĭt sīn′] **53** 24

Express Mail (package)
    [ĭk sprĕs′ māl păk′ ĭj] **46** 23

extension cord [ĭk stĕn′ shən körd′]
    36 5

eye [ī] **5**

eye drops [ī′ drŏps′] **41** 10

eye shadow [ī′ shă′ dō] **23** 30

eyebrow [ī′ brow′] **5** 44

eyebrow pencil [ī′ brow pĕn′ səl]
    23 26

eyelashes [ī′ lăsh′ əz] **5** 46

eyelid [ī′ lĭd′] **5** 45

eyeliner [ī′ lī′ nər] **23** 33

fabric softener [făb′ rĭk sö′ fə nər]
    35 27

face [fās] **4** 1

face guard [fās′ gärd′] **92** 15

factory work [făk′ tə rē würk′] **85**

fairway [fër′ wā′] **95** 12

fall [föl] **96** 7

Fall [föl] **26**

family [făm′ ə lē] **3**

family restaurant [făm′ ə lē rĕs′ tər ənt]
    16

fan belt [făn′ bĕlt′] **51** 53

fare [fër] **55** 21

fare box [fër′ bŏks′] **54** 5

farmhouse [färm′ hows′] **81** 3

farmer [fär′ mər] **81** 7

farming [fär′ mĭng] **81**

fashion designer [făsh′ ən də zī′ nər]
    86 6

father [fŏdh′ ər] **3** 5

faucet [fö′ sĭt] **34** 17, 18

fawn [fön] **67** 27

feather [fĕdh′ ər] **64** 7a

feather duster [fĕdh′ ər dŭs′ tər] **35** 2

fence [fĕns] **81** 9

fender [fĕn′ dər] **52** 10

ferry [fër′ ē] **58** 17

fever [fē′ vər] **40** 2

field [fēld] **81** 16

fields and courses [fēldz′ ənd kör′ səz]
    95

fig [fĭg] **9** 21

fighter plane [fī′ tər plăn′] **48** 1

file cabinet [fīl′ kăb′ ə nət] **83** 21

file clerk [fīl′ klürk′] **83** 23

file folder [fīl′ fōl′ dər] **83** 22

filet [fĭ lā′] **11** 28

fill [fĭl] **26** 9

film [fĭlm] **100** 10, **100** 17

filter paper [fĭl′ tər pā′ pər] **78** 16

fin [fĭn] **65** 3b

finger [fĭng′ gər] **4** 25

fingernail [fĭng′ gər nāl′] **4** 23

fingerprints [fĭng′ gər prĭnts′] **43** 24

finish line [fĭn′ ĭsh līn′] **95** 21

fire [fīr] **28** 9, **42** 5

fire engine [fīr′ ĕn′ jən] **42** 2

fire escape [fīr′ ə skāp′] **42** 4

fire extinguisher
    [fīr′ ĭk stĭng′ gwĭ shər] **42** 11

fire fighter [fīr′ fī′ tər] **42** 10

fire hydrant [fīr′ hī′ drənt] **42** 9

fire truck [fīr′ trŭk′] **42** 3

firefighting [fīr′ fī′ tĭng] **42**

firefly [fīr′ flī′] **63** 17

fireplace [fīr/ plās/] **28** 8

first baseman [fürst/ bās/ mən] **93** 8

first quarter [fürst/ kwör/ tər] **74** 23

fish [fĭsh] **11** 26, **65**

fisherman [fĭsh/ ər mən] **58** 2

fishing [fĭsh/ ĭng] **88**

fishing boat [fĭsh/ ĭng bōt/] **58** 1

fishing line [fĭsh/ ĭng līn/] **88** 8

fishing net [fĭsh/ ĭng nĕt/] **88** 9

fishing rod [fĭsh/ ĭng rŏd/] **88** 7

flag [flăg] **76** 1, **82** 20, **95** 9

flame [flām] **29** 26, **78** 21

flamingo [flə mĭng/ gō] **64** 29

flanker [flăng/ kər] **93** 31

flannel shirt [flăn/ əl shürt/] **19** 3

flare [flër] **51** 41

flash [flăsh] **100** 7

flashlight [flăsh/ līt/] **35** 3

flask [flăsk] **78** 2

(flat) sheet [flăt/ shēt/] **32** 19

flatbed [flăt/ bĕd/] **49** 18

flight attendant [flīt/ ə tĕn/ dənt] **56** 20

flight deck [flīt/ dĕk/] **75** 10

flight engineer [flīt/ ĕn jə nïr/] **56** 17

flipper [flĭp/ ər] **68** 12a

flippers [flĭp/ ərz] **91** 36

floor [flör] **32** 29

Florida [flör/ ə də] **72** 9

florist [flör/ ĭst] **84** 11

flounder [flown/ dər] **65** 7

flowers [flow/ ərz] **60**

flute [flōot] **99** 13

fly [flī] **63** 18

flying mammal [flī/ ĭng mă/ məlz] **66**

foal [fōl] **67** 22

foggy [fŏg/ ē] **25** 12

fold [fōld] **38** 1

food [fōod] **6-18**

foot [fŏot] **5**

football [fŏot/ böl/] **92, 92** 13

football field [fŏot/ böl fēld/] **93**

forceps [för/ səps] **78** 28

forearm [för/ ärm/] **4** 9

forehead [för/ hĕd/] **4** 32

forelegs [för/ lĕgz/] **66** 3d

foreman [för/ mən] **85** 13

fork [förk] **29** 12

forklift [förk/ lĭft/] **58** 4

foul line [fowl/ līn/] **93** 9

foundation [fown dā/ shən] **82** 11

four-door hatchback [för/ dör hăch/ băk] **51**

fox [fŏks] **68** 6

fractions [frăk/ shənz] **79**

frame [frām] **28** 4

frame backpack [frām/ băk/ păk] **89** 28

freezer [frē/ zər] **14** 3, **30** 20

freezing [frē/ zĭng] **25** 11

french fries [frĕnch/ frīz/] **18** 28

French horn [frĕnch/ hörn/] **98** 26

fried chicken [frīd/ chĭk/ ən] **18** 29

Frisbee™ [frĭz/ bē] **90** 13

frog [frŏg] **65** 17

from [frŭm] **103** 10

front bumper [frŭnt/ bŭm/ pər] **51** 51

frozen foods [frō/zən fōodz/] **14** 2

fruit and vegetable market [frōot/ ənd vĕj/ tə bəl mär/ kət] **45** 28

fruit tree [frōot/ trē/] **81** 2

fruits [frōots] **8**

fry [frī] **31** 15

frying pan [frī/ ĭng păn/] **30** 5

fuel truck [fyōo/ əl trŭk/] **49** 3

full moon [fŏol/ mōon/] **74** 24

full slip [fŏol/ slĭp/] **22** 10

fullback [fŏol/ băk/] **93** 34

funnel [fŭn/ əl] **78** 17

fuselage [fyōo/ sə lŏj/] **57** 14

galaxy [găl/ ək sē] **74** 1

Ganges River [găn/ jēz rĭv/ ər] **71** 67

gangway [găng/ wā/] **58** 20

garage [gə rŏj/] **27** 2

garbage can [gär/ bĭj kăn/] **35** 31

garbage truck [gär/ bĭj trŭk/] **49** 6

garden hose [gär/ dən hōs/] **27** 14

gardener [gärd/ nər] **85** 3

gardenia [gär dēn/ yə] **60** 14

garlic [gär/ lĭk] **7** 25

garment bag [gär/ mənt băg/] **56** 1

garter belt [gär/ tər bĕlt/] **22** 14

(garter) snake [gär/ tər snāk/] **65** 9

gas gauge [găs/ gāj/] **50** 9

gas pump [găs/ pŭmp/] **53** 14

gas tank [găs/ tănk/] **50** 34

gas(oline) [găs/ ə lēn/] **80** 28

(gauze) bandage [göz/ băn/ dĭj] **39** 24

gauze pads [göz/ pădz/] **39** 25

gavel [găv/ əl] **43** 12

gear [gïr] **89** 27

gear changer [gïr/ chān/ jər] **52** 22

gearshift [gïr/ shĭft/] **50** 17

geometrical figures [jē/ ə mĕ/ trĭ kəl fĭg/ yərz] **79**

Georgia [jör/ jə] **72** 10

geyser [gī/ zər] **80** 5

gibbon [gĭb/ ən] **69** 15

gill [gĭl] **65** 3c

giraffe [jə răf/] **67** 29

girdle [gür/ dəl] **22** 15

girl [gürl] **2** 9

girl's frame [gürlz/ frām/] **52** 3

give [gĭv] **17** 9

glass [glăs] **12** 20

glasses [glăs/ əz] **21** 44

glider [glī/ dər] **57** 4

globe [glōb] **47** 19

glove [glŭv] **92** 12, **94** 11, **94** 15

glove compartment [glŭv/ kəm pärt/ mənt] **50** 20

gloves [glŭvz] **19** 1

glue [glōo] **37** 33, **76** 17

goal [gōl] **92** 25

goalie [gōl/ ē] **92** 24

goalpost [gōl/ pōst/] **93** 35

goat [gōt] **67** 28

Gobi Desert [gō/ bē dĕz/ ərt] **71** 54

golf [gŏlf] **94**

golf bag [gŏlf/ băg/] **95** 7

golf ball [gŏlf/ böl/] **94** 7

golf cart [gŏlf/ kärt/] **95** 8

golf course [gŏlf/ körs/] **95**

golfer [gŏl/ fər] **94** 10

goose [gōos] **64** 26

gooseberries [gōos/ bër/ ēz] **8** 11

gopher [gō/ fər] **66** 8

gorilla [gə rĭl/ ə] **69** 17

graduated cylinder [grăj/ ōo ā tĭd sĭl/ ən dər] **78** 25

grains [grānz] **60**

granddaughter [grănd/ dö/ tər] **2** 11

grandfather [grănd/ fŏ/ dhər] **3** 2

grandmother [grănd/ mŭ/ dhər] **3** 1

grandparents [grănd păr/ ənts] **2** 10

grandson [grănd/ sŭn/] **2** 12

grapefruit [grăp′frōot′] **8** 7

grapes [grāps] **8** 1

graph paper [grăf′ pā′ pər] **78** 11

grass [grăs] **27** 15

grasses [grăs′əz] **60**

grasshopper [grăs′hŏp′ər] **63** 6

grate [grāt] **31** 2

Great Sandy Desert
[grāt′ săn′ dē dĕz′ ərt] **71** 55

green [grēn] **95** 10

greengrocer [grēn′grō′sər] **84** 7

grill [grĭl] **27** 22, **88** 12

grizzly bear [grĭz′ lē bër′] **69** 23

groceries [grō′sə rēz] **15** 24

ground beef [grownd′ bēf′] **10** 2

grounding plug [grown′ dĭng plŭg′]
36 7

guitar [gĭ tär′] **98** 11

Gulf of Alaska [gŭlf′əv ə lăs′kə]
70 17

Gulf of Guinea [gŭlf′ əv gĭn′ ē] **70** 25

Gulf of Mexico [gŭlf′ əv mĕk sə kō]
70 19

gulfs [gŭlfs] **70**

gun [gŭn] **43** 7

gun turret [gŭn′ tür′ ət] **48** 12

gutter [gŭt′ər] **27** 10, **94** 3

gymnast [jĭm′ nəst] **94** 23

gymnastics [jĭm năs′ tĭks] **94**

hacksaw [hăk′ sö′] **36** 18

hair [hër] **4** 30

hair dryer [hër′ drī′ ər] **34** 26

hairbrush [hër′ brŭsh′] **32** 7

hairdresser [hër′ drĕs′ ər] **84** 10

half (1/2) [hăf] **79** 30

half slip [hăf′ slĭp′] **22** 8

halfback [hăf′ băk′] **93** 33

hall [höl] **76** 12

ham [hăm] **10** 12

hamburger [hăm′bür′ gər] **18** 9

hammer [hăm′ ər] **36** 13

hammock [hăm′ ək] **27** 11

hamper [hăm′ pər] **34** 28

hand [hănd] **4**

hand brake [hănd′ brāk′] **52** 24

hand grenade [hănd′ grə nād′] **48** 29

hand towel [hănd′ tow′ əl] **34** 23

hand truck [hănd′ trŭk′] **87** 4

handball [hănd′ böl′] **94, 94** 12

handcuffs [hănd′ kŭfs′] **43** 4

handicrafts [hăn′ dē krăfts′] **101**

handlebars [hăn′ dəl bärz′] **52** 2

hang [hăng] **38** 6

hang glider [hăng′ glī′ dər] **57** 6

hangar [hăng′ ər] **57** 17

hanger [hăng′ ər] **32** 2

hard hat [härd′ hăt′] **21** 28, **82** 4

harmonica [här mŏn′ ə kə] **98** 30

harness [här′ nəs] **89** 22

harp [härp] **98** 6

hat [hăt] **19** 18

hatchback [hăch′ băk′] **51** 43

hatchet [hăch′ ət] **36** 17

Hawaii [hə wŏ′ ē] **72** 11

hawk [hök] **64** 7

hay [hā] **81** 13

hazelnut(s) [hā′ zəl nŭt(s)′] **9** 30

head [hĕd] **4, 37** 42a

(head of) cauliflower
[hĕd′ əv köl ə flow′ ər] **6** 1

head protector [hĕd prə tĕk′ tər] **94** 14

headache [hĕd′ āk′] **40** 6

headboard [hĕd′ börd′] **32** 14

headlights [hĕd′ līts′] **51** 48

headphones [hĕd′ fōnz′] **100** 29

headrest [hĕd′ rĕst′] **50** 35

headset [hĕd′ sĕt′] **83** 2

heart [härt] **5** 64

heat [hēt] **80** 27

heating pad [hē′ tĭng păd′] **41** 3

hedge clippers [hĕj′ klĭp′ ərz] **27** 29

heel [hēl] **5** 50, **20** 5

heels [hēlz] **20** 25

height [hīt] **79** 34

helicopter [hĕl′ ə kŏp′ tər] **57** 2

helmet [hĕl′ mət] **42** 12, **52** 7, **92** 14

hem [hĕm] **101** 11

hem binding [hĕm′ bīn′ dĭng] **101** 12

herb(s) [ürb(z)] **6** 9

(herd of) cattle [hürd′ əv kăt′ əl] **81** 20

high [hī] **24** 11

high blood pressure [hī′ blŭd prĕsh′ ər]
40 10

high chair [hī′ chër′] **16** 8

high heels [hī′ hēlz′] **20** 25

highway travel [hī′ wā trăv′ əl] **53**

hikers [hī′ kərz] **88** 2

hiking boots [hī′ kĭng bōots′] **19** 9

hill [hĭl] **88** 4

Himalayas [hĭm′ ə lā′ əz] **70** 47

hind legs [hīnd′ lĕgz′] **66** 3b

hip [hĭp] **4** 16

hippopotamus [hĭp′ ə pŏt′ ə məs]
66 14

hit [hĭt] **96** 1

hitchhiker [hĭch′ hī′ kər] **53** 9

hockey stick [hŏk′ ē stĭk′] **92** 18

hog [hög] **66** 30

hold [hōld] **17** 12, **58** 8

hole [hōl] **94** 8

holly [hŏl′ ē] **61** 37

holster [hōl′ stər] **43** 8

home plate [hōm′ plāt′] **93** 15

honeydew melon
[hŭn′ ē dōo mĕl′ ən] **9** 35

hood [hōod] **51** 47

hoof [hōof] **66** 35b

hoofed mammals [hōoft′ măm′ əlz] **66**

hook [hōok] **32** 1, **36** 16

hook and eye [hōok′ ənd ī′] **101** 14

horn [hörn] **50** 12, **52** 5, **66** 16a

horse [hörs] **66** 21

horse racing [hörs′ rā′ sĭng] **94**

horse-drawn carriage
[hörs′ drön kăr′ ĭj] **54** 33

horseback rider [hörs′ băk rī′ dər]
87 6

horses [hörs′ əz] **81** 23

hose [hōz] **42** 8, **50** 57

hot [hŏt] **25** 7

hot air balloon [hŏt′ ër bə lōon′] **57** 1

hot dog [hŏt′ dög′] **18** 2

hot water faucet [hŏt′ wŏt ər fö′ sət]
34 17

house plants [hows′ plănts′] **60** 39

household items [hows′ hōld ī′ təmz]
15 15

household services
[hows′ hōld sür′ və səz] **85**

housekeeper [hows′ kē′ pər] **85** 8

houses [how′ zəz] **27**

housework [hows′ würk′] **38**

Huang River [hwŏng′ riv′ər] **71** 68

hubcap [hŭb′ kăp′] **50** 36

Hudson Bay [hŭd′ sən bā′] **70** 18

human body [hyōō′ mən bŏd′ ē] **4**

hummingbird [hŭm′ ĭng bürd′] **64** 2

hump [hŭmp] **67** 33a

husband [hŭz′ bənd] **2** 3, **3** 12

hyacinth [hī′ə sĭnth] **60** 10

hyena [hī ē′ nə] **68** 30

hypotenuse [hī pŏt′ə nōōs′] **79** 24

ice cream cone [īs′ krēm cōn′] **18** 36

ice hockey [īs′ hŏk′ ē] **92**

ice pack [īs′ păk′] **41** 4

ice skates [īs′ skāts′] **19** 15

ice skating [īs′ skā′ tĭng] **94**

ice tray [īs′ trā′] **30** 21

icy [ī′ sē] **25** 16

Idaho [ī′ də hō′] **72** 12

ignition [ĭg nĭsh′ ən] **50** 14

iguana [ĭ gwŏ′ nə] **65** 13

Illinois [ĭl′ ə noy′] **72** 13

in [ĭn] **102** 7

in front of [ĭn frŭnt′ əv] **102** 6

in-box [ĭn′ bŏks] **83** 12

(index) finger [ĭn′ dĕks fing′ gər] **4** 25

Indian Ocean [ĭn′ dē ən ō′ shən′] **70** 13

Indiana [ĭn′ dē ăn′ ə] **72** 14

individual sports
   [ĭn′ də vĭj′ ōō əl spörts′] **94**

infection [ĭn fĕk′ shən] **40** 14

inflatable raft [ĭn flā′ tə bəl răft′] **59** 20

information desk
   [ĭn′ fər mā′ shən dĕsk′] **47** 22

injection [ĭn jĕk′ shən] **41** 8

injuries [ĭn′ jə rēz] **40**

insect bite [ĭn′ sĕkt bīt′] **40** 3

insects [ĭn′ sĕkts] **63**

instep [ĭn′ stĕp′] **5** 51

instruments [ĭn′ strə mənts]
   39 13, **56** 14, **98**

internal organs [ĭn tür′ nəl ör′ gənz] **5**

intersection [ĭn′ tər sĕk′ shən] **44** 11

interstate highway
   [ĭn′ tər stāt hī′ wā] **53** 1

intestines [ĭn tĕs′ tənz] **5** 67

into [ĭn′ tōō] **103** 12

Iowa [ī′ə wə] **72** 15

iris [ī′ rəs] **5** 47, **60** 11

iron (n) [ī′ ərn] **35** 12

iron (v) [ī′ ərn] **38** 11

ironing board [ī′ ər nĭng börd′] **35** 13

jack [jăk] **32** 26b, **50** 38

jacket [jăk′ ət] **19** 17, **21** 33

jackhammer [jăk′ hăm′ər] **82** 22

jail [jāl] **43** 1

janitor [jăn′ə tər] **85** 9

jar [jär] **12** 9

jaw [jö] **4** 38

jeans [jēnz] **19** 6

jeep [jēp] **48** 9

jelly [jĕl′ ē] **18** 31

jellyfish [jĕl′ ē fĭsh′] **62** 12

jet engine [jĕt′ ĕn′ jən] **57** 11

jet fuel [jĕt′ fyōō′ əl] **80** 31

(jet) plane [jĕt′ plān′] **57** 18

jeweller [jōō′ ə lər] **84** 12

jewelry [jōō′ əl rē] **23**

jewelry box [jōō′ əl rē bŏks′] **32** 4

jigsaw [jĭg′ sö] **36** 3

jockey [jŏk′ ē] **94** 21

jogging path [jŏg′ ĭng păth′] **87** 9

judge [jŭj] **43** 10

jukebox [jōōk′ bŏks′] **16** 12

jump [jŭmp] **96** 8

jungle gym [jŭng′ əl jĭm′] **87** 17

Jupiter [jōō′ pə tər] **74** 15

jury [jōōr′ ē] **43** 21

jury box [joor′ ē bŏks′] **43** 20

kangaroo [kăng′ gə rōō′] **66** 3

Kansas [kăn′ zəs] **72** 16

Kara Sea [kär′ ə sē′] **70** 31

kayak [kī′ ăk] **59** 17

Kentucky [kĕn tŭk′ ē] **72** 17

ketchup [kĕch′ əp] **16** 4

kettledrum [kĕt′ əl drŭm′] **98** 21

keyboard [kē′ börd′] **98** 1a, **100** 33

keyboard player [kē′ börd plā′ ər] **99** 22

kickstand [kĭk′ stănd′] **52** 9

kidney [kĭd′ nē] **5** 70

kidney bean(s) [kĭd′ nē bēn(z)′] **6** 13

kitchen [kĭch′ ən] **30**

kite [kīt] **91** 22

kitten [kĭt′ ən] **68** 5

knee [nē] **4** 19

knee socks [nē′ sŏks′] **22** 16

knife [nīf] **29** 15

knitting [nĭt′ ĭng] **101** 22

knitting needle [nĭt′ ĭng nē′ dəl] **101** 25

knuckle [nŭk′ əl] **4** 22

koala [kō ŏl′ ə] **66** 1

label [lā′ bəl] **46** 21

lacrosse [lə krös′] **92**

lacrosse stick [lə krös′ stĭk′] **92** 16

ladder [lăd′ ər] **42** 1, **82** 8

ladybug [lā′ dē bŭg′] **63** 14

lamb [lăm] **10** 13, **67** 24

lamp [lămp] **28** 28

lampshade [lămp′ shād′] **28** 27

landing gear [lăn′ dĭng gïr′] **57** 15

lane [lān] **94** 4

lantern [lăn′ tərn] **88** 29

lapel [lə pĕl′] **20** 1

Laptev Sea [lăp′ tĕv sē′] **70** 33

last quarter [lăst′ kwör′ tər] **74** 25

launchpad [lönch′ păd′] **75** 15

laundry [lön′ drē] **35** 28

laundry basket [lön′ drē băs′ kət] **35** 29

laundry detergent [lön′ drē də tür′ jənt]
   35 25

lawn mower [lön′ mō′ ər] **27** 12

lead guitarist [lēd′ gĭ tär′ ĭst] **99** 25

leaf [lēf] **60** 36a

leave [lēv] **77** 13

left fielder [lĕft′ fēl′ dər] **93** 1

left guard [lĕft′ gärd′] **93** 26

left lane [lĕft′ lān′] **53** 5

left tackle [lĕft′ tăk′ əl] **93** 25

leg [lĕg] **4** 17, **10** 14, **11** 20

(legal) pad [lē′ gəl păd′] **83** 26

lemon [lĕm′ ən] **8** 9

Lena River [lē′ nə rĭv′ ər] **71** 66

length [lĕngth] **79** 36

lens [lĕnz] **100** 6

leopard [lĕp′ərd] **68** 1

letter [lĕt′ər] **46** 7

letter carrier [lĕt′ər kăr′ yər] **46** 3

lettuce [lĕt′əs] **6** 6

level [lĕv′əl] **82** 3

librarian [lī brër′ ē ən] **47** 23

library card [lī′ brër ē kärd′] **47** 3

library clerk [lī′ brër ē klürk′] **47** 1

license plate [lī′ səns plāt′] **50** 28

lid [lĭd] **30** 9

life jacket [līf′ jăk′ ət] **59** 1

life preserver [līf′ prə zür′ vər] **90** 9

lifeboat [līf′ bōt′] **58** 19, **90** 10

lifeguard [līf′ gärd′] **90** 6
lifeguard chair [līf′ gärd chër′] **90** 8
light (v) [līt] **17** 13
light (adj) [līt] **24** 9
light switch [līt′ swĭch′] **32** 25
lightbulb [līt′ bŭlb′] **35** 22
lighter [lī′ tər] **16** 30
lighthouse [līt′ hows′] **58** 14
lily [lĭl′ ē] **60** 3
lima bean(s) [lī′ mə bēn(z)′] **6** 16
lime [līm] **8** 10
line [līn] **58** 25
lines [līnz] **79**
linesman [līnz′ mən] **82** 17
lion [lī′ ən] **68** 3
lip [lĭp] **4** 43
lipstick [lĭp′ stĭk′] **23** 29
liquor (bottle) [lĭk′ ər bŏt′ əl] **16** 22
listen [lĭs′ ən] **77** 6
little finger [lĭt′ əl fĭng′ gər] **4** 28
little league baseball [lĭt′ əl lēg bās′ böl]
     92
Little Leaguer [lĭt′ əl lēg′ ər] **92** 8
little toe [lĭt′ əl tō′] **5** 55
liver [lĭv′ ər] **5** 65
livestock [līv′ stŏk′] **81** 12
living quarters [lĭv′ ĭng kwör′ tərz]
     75 11
living room [lĭv′ ĭng rōōm′] **28**
lizard [lĭz′ ərd] **65** 15
llama [lŏm′ ə] **66** 15
loaf [lōf] **12** 7
loafer [lō′ fər] **21** 42
lobby [lŏb′ ē] **44** 2
lobster [lŏb′ stər] **11** 30, **62** 13
lock [lŏk] **52** 13
locker [lŏk′ ər] **76** 6
locksmith [lŏk′ smĭth′] **85** 4
log [lög] **28** 10
long [löng] **24** 2
long johns [löng′ jŏnz′] **22** 7
long sleeve [löng′ slēv′] **20** 15
loose [lōōs] **24** 4
(loose-leaf) paper [lōōs′ lēf pā′ pər]
     76 13
loudspeaker [lowd′ spē′ kər] **76** 3
Louisiana [lōō ē ′ zē ăn′ ə] **72** 18
lounge chair [lownj′ chër′] **27** 24

low [lō] **24** 12
lunar eclipse [lōō′ nər ĭ klĭps′] **74** 6
lunar module [lōō′ nər mŏj′ ōōl] **75** 7
lunch box [lŭnch′ bŏks′] **20** 31
lunch truck [lŭnch′ trŭk′] **49** 8
lung [lŭng] **5** 63
machine gun [mə shēn′ gŭn′] **48** 25
magazine [măg′ ə zēn′] **47** 16
magnet [măg′ nət] **78** 27
magnifying glass [măg′ nə fī ĭng glăs′]
     78 15
magnolia [măg nōl′ yə] **61** 29
mail [māl] **46** 2
mail slot [māl′ slŏt′] **46** 13
mail truck [māl′ trŭk′] **46** 5
mailbag [māl′ băg′] **46** 4
mailbox [māl′ bŏks′] **46** 1
Maine [mān] **72** 19
maintenance [mān′ tə nəns] **85**
make (the bed) [māk′ dhə bĕd′] **38** 8
makeup [māk′ ŭp′] **23**
mallet [măl′ ĭt] **36** 11
mammals [măm′ əlz] **66-69**
man [măn] **2** 2
manager [măn′ ĭ jər] **83** 18
mandolin [măn′ də lĭn′] **98** 4
mane [mān] **66** 21a
mango [măng′ gō] **8** 5
manhole [măn′ hōl′] **45** 32
mantel [măn′ təl] **28** 7
mantis [măn′ tĭs] **63** 7
manual transmission
     [măn′ yōō əl trănz mĭsh′ ən] **50**
map [măp] **70**
maple [mā′ pəl] **61** 38
marigold [măr′ ə gōld′] **60** 6
marine [mə rēn′] **48** 18
Marines [mə rēnz′] **48** 17
Mars [märz] **74** 14
Maryland [mër′ ə lənd] **72** 20
mascara [mă skăr′ ə] **23** 28
mashed potatoes [măsht′ pə tā tōz′]
     18 17
mask [măsk] **91** 35
Massachusetts [măs′ ə chōō′ sĭts]
     72 21
mast [măst] **59** 8
mat [măt] **50** 22

matches [măch′ əz] **16** 28
material [mə tĭr′ ē əl] **101** 4
math [măth] **79**
mattress [mă′ trəs] **32** 17
measurement [mĕzh′ ər mənt] **79**
meat [mēt] **10**
meatballs [mēt′ bölz′] **18** 11
mechanic [mə kăn′ ĭk] **84** 2
media [mē′ dē ə] **86**
medical care [mĕd′ ə kəl kër′] **39**
medicine [mĕd′ ə sən] **41**
medicine chest [mĕd′ ə sən chĕst′]
     34 14
medicine dropper [mĕd′ ə sən drŏp′ ər]
     78 26
Mediterranean Sea
     [mĕd′ ĭ tə rā′ nē ən sē′] **70** 24
melon [mĕl′ ən] **9** 35
menu [mĕn′ yōō] **16** 7
Mercury [mür′ kyə rē] **74** 11
merry-go-round [mër′ ē gō rownd′]
     87 5
message pad [mĕs′ ĭj păd′] **83** 25
messenger [mĕs′ ən jər] **86** 19
metal detector [mĕt′ əl də tĕk′ tər]
     56 10
meteor [mē′ tē ər] **74** 5
meter [mē′ tər] **55** 23
mezzanine [mĕz′ ə nēn′] **99** 13
Michigan [mĭsh′ ə gən] **72** 22
microfilm [mī′ krə fĭlm′] **47** 13
microfilm reader [mī′ krə fĭlm rē′ dər]
     47 14
microscope [mī′ krə skōp′] **78** 30
microwave oven [mī′ krə wāv ŭv′ ən]
     30 23
middle finger [mĭd′ əl fĭng′ gər] **4** 26
milk [mĭlk] **14** 5
Minicam™ [mĭn′ ē kăm′] **100** 2
Minnesota [mĭn′ ə sō′ tə] **72** 23
mirror [mïr′ ər] **32** 5
Mississippi [mĭs′ ə sĭp′ ē] **72** 24
Mississippi River [mĭs′ ə sĭp′ ē rĭv′ ər]
     71 58
Missouri [mĭ zōōr′ ē] **73** 25
mitt [mĭt] **27** 20
mittens [mĭt′ ənz] **19** 11

mixed vegetables [mĭkst′ věj′ tə bəlz] **18** 16

mixing bowl [mĭk′ sĭng bōl′] **30** 24

mobile [mō′ bēl] **33** 2

model [mŏd′ əl] **86** 5

Mojave Desert [mō hŏv′ ē děz′ ərt] **71** 48

money [mŭn′ ē] **12**

money order [mŭn′ ē ör′ dər] **46** 18

monitor [mŏn′ ə tər] **100** 32

monkey [mŭng′ ke] **69** 14

monkey wrench [mŭng′ kē rěnch′] **36** 12

monorail [mŏn′ ə rāl′] **55** 29

Montana [mŏn tăn′ ə] **73** 26

Moon [mōōn] **74** 9

mooring [mōōr′ ĭng] **59** 19

moose [mōōs] **67** 35

mop [mŏp] **35** 6

(mop) refill [mŏp′ rē′ fĭl] **35** 11

mortar [mör′ tər] **48** 28

mosquito [mə skē′ tō] **63** 13

motel [mō těl′] **90** 3

moth [mŏth] **63** 21

mother [mŭdh′ ər] **3** 4

motor oil [mōt′ ər oyl′] **80** 33

motor scooter [mōt′ ər skōō′ tər] **52** 29

motorboat [mōt′ ər bōt′] **59** 13

motorcycle [mōt′ ər sī′ kəl] **52** 30, **53** 19

mountain [mown′ tən] **89** 19

mountain climbing [mown′ tən klīm′ ĭng] **89**

mountain ranges [mown′ tən rān′ jəz] **71**

mouse [mows] **66** 9

mousetrap [mows′ trăp′] **35** 32

mouth [mowth] **4** 2

mover [mōō′ vər] **49** 12

movie camera [mōō′ vē kăm′ ə rə] **100** 15

moving van [mōō′ vĭng văn′] **49** 11

mow [mō] **26** 6

mum [mŭm] **60** 4

muscle [mŭs′ əl] **5** 62

mushroom(s) [mŭsh′ rōōm(z)] **7** 30

music [myōō′ zĭk] **99**

musical comedy [myōō′ zə kəl kŏm′ ə dē] **99**

musical instruments [myōō′ zə kəl ĭn′ strə mənts] **98**

musician [myōō zĭsh′ ən] **99** 10

mussel(s) [mŭs′ əl(z)] **11** 34, **62** 3

mustache [mŭs′ tăsh] **4** 40

mustard [mŭs′ tərd] **18** 1

nail [nāl] **37** 41

nail clippers [nāl′ klĭp′ ərz] **23** 31

nail polish [nāl′ pŏl′ ĭsh] **23** 25

nailbrush [nāl′ brŭsh′] **34** 20

napkin [năp′ kĭn] **29** 14

natural gas [năch′ ər əl găs′] **80** 29

Navy [nā′ vē] **48** 13

Nebraska [nə brăs′ kə] **73** 27

neck [něk] **4** 4

necklace [něk′ lĭs] **23** 6

nectarine [něk′ tə rēn′] **8** 17

needle [nē′ dəl] **39** 26, **60** 34a, **101** 18

needlecrafts [nē′ dəl krăfts′] **101**

needlepoint [nē′ dəl poynt′] **101** 26

neighborhood parks [nā′ bər hŏŏd pärks′] **87**

nephew [něf′ yōō] **3** 13

Neptune [něp′ tōōn] **74** 18

nest [něst] **64** 31

net [nět] **92** 23

Nevada [nə văd′ ə] **73** 28

new [nōō] **24** 13

New Hampshire [nōō′ hămp′ shər] **72** 29

New Jersey [nōō′ jür′ ze] **73** 30

New Mexico [nōō′ měk′ sə kō] **73** 31

new moon [nōō′ mōōn′] **74** 26

New York [nōō′ york′] **73** 32

newscaster [nōōz′ kăs′ tər] **86** 2

newspaper [nōōz′ pā′ pər] **21** 48

newsstand [nōōz′ stănd′] **45** 30

next to [někst′ tōō] **102** 11

nickel [nĭk′ əl] **13** 28

niece [nēs] **3** 14

Niger River [nī′ jər rĭv′ ər] **71** 61

night table [nīt′ tā′ bəl] **32** 27

nightgown [nīt′ gown′] **22** 21

nightstick [nīt′ stĭk′] **43** 9

Nile River [nīl′ rĭv′ ər] **71** 63

nipple [nĭp′ əl] **33** 18

north [nörth] **71** 71

North America [nörth′ ə mër′ ə kə] **70** 1

North Atlantic [nörth′ ăt lăn′ tĭk] **70** 11

North Carolina [nörth′ kăr ə lī′ nə] **73** 33

North Dakota [nörth′ də kō′ tə] **73** 34

North Pacific [nörth′ pə sĭf′ ĭk] **70** 9

North Sea [nörth′ sē′] **70** 21

nose [nōz] **4** 36, **57** 8

nostril [nŏs′ trĭl] **4** 37

nozzle [nŏz′ əl] **42** 17

nuclear reactor [nōō′ klē ər rē ăk′ tər] **80** 13

nurse [nürs] **39** 19

nut [nŭt] **37** 39

nuts [nŭts] **9**

oak [ōk] **61** 33

oar [ör] **59** 22

oarlock [ör′ lŏk′] **59** 21

oats [ōts] **60** 23

Ob River [ŏb′ rĭv′ ər] **71** 64

oboe [ō′ bō] **98** 15

obtuse angle [ŏb tōōs′ ăng′ gəl] **79** 5

occupations [ŏk′ yə pā′ shənz] **84-86**

ocean liner [ō′ shən lī′ nər] **58** 27

oceans [ō′ shənz] **70**

octopus [ŏk′ tə pəs] **62** 6

office [ö′ fĭs] **83**

office building [ö′ fĭs bĭl′ dĭng] **44** 1

officer [ö′ fĭ sər] **86** 13

Ohio [ō hī′ ō] **73** 35

oil [oyl] **38** 12

oil well [oyl′ wěl′] **80** 1

ointment [oynt′ mənt] **41** 9

Oklahoma [ō′ klə hō′ mə] **73** 36

old [ōld] **24** 14

on [ŏn] **102** 5

on top of [ŏn tŏp′ əv] **102** 10

onion(s) [ŭn′ yən(z)] **7** 31

open [ō′ pən] **24** 15, **31** 3

optician [ŏp tĭsh′ ən] **84** 9

oral hygienist [ör′ əl hī jē′ nĭst] **39** 14

orange [ör′ ĭnj] **8** 8

orangutan [ə răng′ ə tăn′] **69** 18

orbit [ör′ bĭt] **74** 21

orchard [ör′ chərd] **81** 1

orchestra [ör′ kə strə] **99** 6

orchestra seating [ör′kə strə sēt′ĭng] **99** 12

orchid [ör′kĭd] **60** 12

order [ör′dər] **17** 5

Oregon [ör′ə gən] **73** 37

organ [ör′gən] **98** 29

ostrich [ŏs′trĭch] **64** 12

otter [ŏt′ər] **68** 10

out of [owt′əv] **103** 7

outboard motor [owt′börd mō′tər] **59** 12

outer space [owt′ər spās′] **74**

outlet [owt′lət] **36** 6

oval [ō′vəl] **79** 18

oven [ŭv′ən] **30** 32

over [ō′vər] **103** 8

overalls [ō′vər ölz′] **21** 30

overcoat [ō′vər kōt′] **19** 20

overhead projector
[ō′vər hĕd prə jĕk′tər] **76** 27

overpass [ō′vər păs′] **53** 3

owl [owl] **64** 6

oyster(s) [oy′stər(z)] **11** 33, **62** 2

pacifier [păs′ə fī′ər] **33** 22

pack [păk] **13** 16

package [păk′ĭj] **12** 4, **46** 19

pad [păd] **83** 26

paddle [păd′əl] **59** 3, **94** 18

pail [pāl] **90** 16

paint (v) [pānt] **26** 1

paint (n) [pānt] **37** 31

paintbrush [pānt′brŭsh′] **37** 30

Painted Desert [pān′təd dez′ərt] **71** 49

painter [pān′tər] **85** 7

painting [pān′tĭng] **28** 5

(pair of) scissors [pĕr′əv sĭz′ərz]
101 17

pajamas [pə jŏm′əz] **22** 19

palm [pŏm] **4** 29, **61** 26

pan [păn] **37** 28

pancakes [păn′kāks′] **18** 5

pancreas [pang′krē əs] **5** 71

panda [păn′də] **69** 20

panel truck [păn′əl trŭk′] **49** 9

pansy [păn′zē] **60** 2

panties [păn′tēz] **22** 11

pants [pănts] **21** 27

pantyhose [păn′tē hōz′] **22** 5

papaya [pə pī′yə] **8** 6

paper [pā′pər] **76** 13

paper clips [pā′pər klĭps′] **83** 28

paper towels [pā′pər tow′əlz] **35** 23

parachute [păr′ə shoot′] **48** 6

parakeet [păr′ə kēt] **64** 15

parallel lines [păr′ə lĕl līnz′] **79** 4

paramedic [păr′ə mĕd′ĭk] **42** 7

Parana River [păr′ə nŏ′rĭv′ər] **71** 60

parents [păr′ənts] **2** 6

park [pärk] **87**

park ranger [pärk′rān′jər] **88** 5

parka [pär′kə] **19** 8

parking lights [pär′kĭng līts′] **51** 49

parking garage [pär′kĭng gə rŏj′]
45 19

parking meter [pär′kĭng mē′tər]
45 20

parrot [păr′ət] **64** 16

part [pärt] **4** 31

pass [păs] **96** 5

passenger [păs′ĭn jər] **55** 25

passenger car [păs′ĭn jər kär′] **53** 15

pasture [păs′chər] **81** 6

patient [pā′shənt] **39** 20

patio [păt′ē ō′] **27** 17

pattern [păt′ərn] **101** 7

pattern piece [păt′ərn pēs′] **101** 6

paw [pö] **69** 29a

pay [pā] **17** 7

pea(s) [pē(z)] **6** 17

peach [pēch] **9** 37

peacock [pē′kŏk′] **64** 18

peak [pēk] **89** 20

peanut(s) [pē′nŭt(s)′] **9** 28

pear [pĕr] **8** 18

pedal [pĕd′əl] **39** 18, **52** 19

pedestrian [pə dĕs′trē ən] **44** 12

peel (n) [pēl] **9** 20a

peel (v) [pēl] **31** 5

pegboard [pĕg′börd′] **36** 15

pelican [pĕl′ə kən] **64** 24

pencil [pĕn′səl] **76** 24

pencil eraser [pĕn′səl ə rā′sər] **76** 21

pencil sharpener
[pĕn′səl shär′pə nər] **76** 20, **83** 30

Pennsylvania [pĕn səl vān′yə] **73** 38

penny [pĕn′ē] **13** 27

penguin [pĕn′gwĭn] **64** 27

people [pē′pəl] **2**

pepper shaker [pĕp′ər shā′kər] **29** 9

pepper(s) [pĕp′ər(z)] **7** 22

percussion [pər kŭsh′ən] **98**

perfume [pür′fyoom] **23** 27

periodicals section
[pïr′ē ŏd′ə kəlz sĕk′shən] **47** 15

periscope [pĕr′ə skōp′] **48** 8

perpendicular lines
[pür′pən dĭk′yə lər līnz′] **79** 2

Persian Gulf [pür′zhən gŭlf′] **70** 28

personal computer (PC)
[pür′sə nəl kŭm pyoo′tər]/
[pē′sē′] **100** 31

personnel [pür′sə nĕl′] **48**

petal [pĕt′əl] **60** 18b

petri dish [pēt′rē dĭsh′] **78** 3

petunia [pə toon′yə] **60** 7

pharmacist [fär′mə sĭst] **84** 1

phases of the moon
[fā′zəz əv dhə moon′] **74**

pheasant [fĕz′ənt] **64** 19

Phillips screwdriver
[fĭl′ĭps skroo′drī vər] **37** 25

phone [fōn] **32** 26

photocopier [fō′tə kŏp′ē ər] **83** 24

photocopy machine
[fō tə kŏp ē mə shēn′] **47** 18

photographer [fə tŏg′rə fər] **86** 4

photography [fə tŏg′rə fē] **100**

piano [pē ăn′ō] **98** 1

piccolo [pĭk′ə lō′] **98** 12

pick (v) [pĭk] **26** 7

pick (n) [pĭk] **98** 11a

pickup truck [pĭk′ŭp trŭk′] **49** 4

pickax [pĭk′ăks′] **82** 13

pickle [pĭk′əl] **18** 8

picnic area [pĭk′nĭk ĕr′ē ə] **88**

picnic basket [pĭk′nĭk băs′kət] **88** 13

picnic table [pĭk′nĭk tā′bəl] **88** 15

piece [pēs] **12** 22

pier [pïr] **58** 3

pierced earring [pïrst′ïr′ĭng] **23** 16

pigeon [pĭj′ən] **64** 1

pill [pĭl] **41** 7

pillow [pĭl′ō] **32** 16

pillowcase [pĭl′ō kās′] **32** 15

pilot [pī ́ lət] **56** 15

pin [pǐn] **23** 8, **94** 5, **101** 20

pincushion [pǐn ́ kŏŏsh ́ ən] **101** 3

pine [pīn] **60** 34

pineapple [pīn ́ ăp ́ əl] **8** 4

ping-pong [pǐng ́ pŏng ́] **94**

ping-pong ball [pǐng ́ pŏng böl ́] **94** 19

pinking shears [pǐng ́ kǐng shïrz ́]
101 5

pipe [pīp] **16** 26, **35** 18

pipette [pī pět ́] **78** 14

pit [pǐt] **8** 37a

pitcher [pǐch ́ ər] **29** 4, **93** 12

pitcher's mound [pǐch ́ ərz mownd ́]
93 11

pitchfork [pǐch ́ förk ́] **81** 14

pizza [pēt ́ sə] **18** 30

plaid [plăd] **24** 22

plane [plān] **57** 18

planets [plăn ́ əts] **74**

plant (v) [plănt] **26** 4

plants (n) [plănts] **60**

plate [plāt] **29** 13

plateau [plă tō ́] **88** 1

platform [plăt ́ förm ́] **54** 11

playground [plā ́ grownd ́] **87** 15

playpen [plā ́ pěn ́] **33** 30

pleasure boating [plĕzh ́ ər bō ́ tǐng] **59**

pliers [plī ́ ərz] **36** 19

plug [plŭg] **37** 43d

plum [plŭm] **9** 34

plumber [plŭm ́ ər] **85** 1

plunger [plŭn ́ jər] **35** 14

Pluto [plōō ́ tō] **74** 19

pocket [pŏk ́ ət] **21** 41

pod [pŏd] **6** 17a

podium [pō ́ dē əm] **99** 7

poinsettia [poyn sět ́ē ə] **60** 15

poison ivy [poy ́ zən ī ́ vē] **61** 45

poison oak [poy ́ zən ōk ́] **61** 43

poison sumac [poy ́ zən sōō ́ măk]
61 44

poisonous plants [poy ́ zə nəs plănts ́]
61

polar bear [pōl ́ ər bër ́] **69** 22

pole [pōl] **94** 34, **95** 14

police officer [pə lēs ́ öf ́ ə sər] **43** 6

police station [pə lēs ́ stā ́ shən] **43**

polish [pŏl ́ ǐsh] **38** 3

polka dot [pō ́ kə dŏt ́] **24** 19

pond [pŏnd] **87** 8

pony [pō ́ nē] **67** 20

poplar [pŏp ́ lər] **61** 30

porch [pörch] **27** 6

porcupine [pör ́ kyə pīn ́] **66** 11

pork [pörk] **10** 6

pork chops [pörk ́ chŏps ́] **18** 15

port [pört] **58**

porter [pör ́ tər] **56** 5

porthole [pört ́ hōl ́] **58** 21

post [pōst] **23** 18

post office [pōst ́ öf ́ ǐs] **44** 9, **46**

postal worker [pōs ́ təl wür ́ kər] **46** 14

postcard [pōst ́ kärd ́] **46** 17

postmark [pōst ́ märk ́] **46** 9

pot [pŏt] **30** 13

pot holder [pŏt ́ hōl ́ dər] **30** 34

potato chips [pə tā ́ tō chǐps ́] **18** 4

potato(es) [pə tā ́ tō(z)] **7** 23

potty [pŏt ́ ē] **33** 33

pouch [powch] **66** 3c

pouched mammals [powcht ́ măm ́ əlz]
66

poultry [pōl ́ trē] **10**

pour [pör] **31** 4

power lines [pow ́ ər līnz ́] **80** 24

power sander [pow ́ ər săn ́ dər] **37** 26

power saw [pow ́ ər sö ́] **27** 25

power station [pow ́ ər stā ́ shən] **80** 20

prepositions [prep ́ ə zǐ ́ shənz]
102, **103**

primates [prī ́ māts] **69**

print [prǐnt] **24** 21

printer [prǐn ́ tər] **83** 4

printout [prǐnt ́ owt ́] **83** 8

prints [prǐnts] **100** 11

prism [prǐz ́ əm] **78** 1

private jet [prī ́ vət jět ́] **57** 3

produce [prŏd ́ ōōs] **14** 9

programs [prō ́ grămz] **99** 17

projector [prə jěk ́ tər] **100** 16

propane gas [prō ́ pān găs ́] **80** 30

propeller plane [prə pěl ́ ər plān ́] **57** 7

prosecuting attorney
[prŏ ́ sə kyōō tǐng ə tür ́ nē] **43** 17

prune [prōōn] **9** 22

public library [pŭb ́ lǐk lī ́ brër ē] **47**

public transportation
[pŭb ́ lǐk trăns pər tā ́ shən] **54**

public telephone [pŭb ́ lǐk těl ́ ə fōn]
44 7

puck [pŭk] **92** 17

pump [pŭmp] **13** 14, **52** 21

pumpkin [pŭmp ́ kǐn] **7** 26

punishment [pŭn ́ ǐsh mənt] **43**

pupil [pyōō ́ pəl] **5** 48

puppy [pŭp ́ ē] **69** 27

purse [pürs] **20** 23

push [pŏŏsh] **26** 12

putter [pŭt ́ ər] **94** 9

puzzle [pŭz ́ əl] **33** 31

pyramid [pïr ́ ə mǐd ́] **79** 25

quantities [kwŏn ́ tə tēz] **12**

quarter [kwör ́ tər] **11** 18, **13** 30,
79 31

quarterback [kwör ́ tər băk ́] **93** 32

quill [kwǐl] **66** 11a

quilting [kwǐl ́ tǐng] **101** 32

rabbit [răb ́ ǐt] **66** 13

raccoon [ră kōōn ́] **68** 7

race track [rās ́ trăk ́] **95**

(racing) handlebars
[rā ́ sǐng hăn ́ dəl bärz] **52** 2

rack [răk] **47** 17, **78** 8

racket [răk ́ ǐt] **94** 2

racquet [răk ́ ǐt] **94** 29

racquetball [răk ́ ǐt böl ́] **94** 30

radiator [rā ́ dē āt ́ ər] **51** 56

radio [rā ́ dē ō ́] **50** 18

radish(es) [răd ́ ǐsh (əz)] **7** 29

radius [rā ́ dē əs] **79** 14

raft [răft] **89** 16

rafters [răf ́ tərz] **82** 1

rafting [răf ́ tǐng] **89**

rags [răgz] **35** 4

rain boots [rān ́ bōōts ́] **19** 25

raincoat [rān ́ kōt ́] **21** 38

rainy [rān ́ ē] **25** 1

raise (one's hand) [rāz ́ wŭnz hănd ́]
77 1

raisin(s) [rā ́ zən(z)] **9** 24

rake (v) [rāk] **26** 10

rake (n) [rāk] **27** 30

ranch [rănch] **81**

ranch house [rănch′ hows′] **27**

ranching [rănch′ ĭng] **81**

rapids [răp′ ĭdz] **89** 17

rash [răsh] **40** 1

raspberries [răz′ bĕr′ ēz] **8** 16

rat [răt] **66** 7

rattle [răt′ əl] **33** 21

rattlesnake [răt′ əl snāk′] **65** 10

razor [rā′ zər] **23** 20

razor blades [rā′ zər blādz′] **23** 23

read [rēd] **77** 4

real estate agent [rēl′ ə stāt ā′ jənt]
    85 5

rear bumper [rĭr′ bŭm′ pər] **50** 42

rearview mirror [rĭr′ vyo͞o mĭr′ ər]
    50 7

receipt [rə sēt′] **15** 20, **55** 24

receiver [rə sē′ vər] **100** 21

receptionist [rə sĕp′ shə nəst] **86** 17

recliner [rə klī′ nər] **28** 16

records [rĕk′ ərdz] **100** 23

rectangle [rĕk′ tăng′ gəl] **79** 19

Red Sea [rĕd′ sē′] **70** 29

redwood [rĕd′ wo͝od′] **61** 25

(reel of) film [rēl′ əv fĭlm′] **100** 17

referee [rĕf′ ə rē′] **93** 22, **94** 16

reference section
    [rĕf′ ə rəns sĕk′ shən] **47** 21

(reference) librarian
    [rĕf′ ə rəns lī brĕr′ e ən] **47** 23

refill [rē′ fĭl′] **35** 11

refinery [rə fī′ nə rē] **80** 12

reflector [rə flĕk′ tər] **52** 25

refreshment stand
    [rə frĕsh′ mənt stănd′] **90** 2

refrigerator [rə frĭj′ ə rā′ tər] **30** 19

reins [rānz] **94** 22

relationships [rə lā′ shən shĭps′] **2**

remedies [rĕm′ ə dēz] **41**

remote control [rə mōt′ kən trōl′]
    28 17

repair [rə pĕr′] **38** 10

repairperson [rə pĕr′ pür′ sən] **84** 5

reporter [rə pör′ tər] **86** 11

reptiles [rĕp′ tīlz] **65**

rescue [rĕs′ kyo͞o] **42**

restaurant [rĕs′ tə rənt] **16**

retriever [rə trē′ vər] **69** 26

return address [rə türn′ ă drĕs′] **46** 8

rhinoceros [rī nŏs′ ə rəs] **66** 16

Rhode Island [rōd′ ī′ lənd] **73** 39

rice [rīs] **60** 21

ride [rīd] **97** 13

rider [rī′ dər] **54** 6

rifle [rī′ fəl] **48** 21

right angle [rīt′ ăng′ gəl] **79** 23

right fielder [rīt′ fēl′ dər] **93** 3

right guard [rīt′ gärd′] **93** 28

right lane [rīt′ lān′] **53** 7

right tackle [rīt′ tăk′ əl] **93** 29

right triangle [rīt′ trī′ ăng gəl] **79** 22

rind [rīnd] **8** 8b

ring(s) [rĭng(z)] **23** 2, **74** 16a, **94** 17

ring binder [rĭng′ bīn′ dər] **76** 14

ring finger [rĭng′ fĭng′ gər] **4** 27

ring stand [rĭng′ stănd′] **78** 19

rink [rĭngk] **94** 25

Rio Grande River [rē′ ō grănd′ rĭv′ ər]
    71 57

rivers [rĭv′ ərz] **71**

road sign [rōd′ sīn′] **53** 23

road work [rōd′ würk′] **82**

roadrunner [rōd′ rŭn′ ər] **64** 32

roast [rōst] **10** 3, **10** 8

roasting pan [rōs′ tĭng păn′] **30** 17

robes [rōbz] **43** 11

robin [rŏb′ in] **64** 9

rock group [rŏk′ gro͞op′] **99**

rocket [rŏk′ ət] **75** 13

rocks [rŏks] **88** 11

rocking chair [rŏk′ ĭng chĕr′] **33** 16

Rocky Mountains [rŏk′ ē mown′ tənz]
    71 40

rodents [rō′ dənts] **66**

roll [rōl] **12** 11, **18** 19

(roll of) film [rōl′ əv fĭlm′] **100** 10

roller [rōl′ ər] **37** 29

rolling pin [rōl′ ĭng pĭn′] **30** 25

rolodex [rōl′ ə dĕks′] **83** 14

rooster [ro͞o′ stər] **64** 21

roof [ro͞of] **27** 4

root [ro͞ot] **60** 35d

rope [rōp] **89** 23

rose [rōz] **60** 18

rotor [rō′ tər] **57** 2a

rough [rŭf] **95** 6

router [row′ tər] **37** 37

row [rō] **47** 11, **81** 18

rowboat [rō′ bōt′] **59** 23

Rub′ al Khali Desert
    [ro͞ob′ ăl kŏl′ ē dĕz′ ərt] **71** 52

rubber tubing [rŭb′ ər to͞ob′ ĭng] **78** 18

rudder [rŭd′ ər] **59** 5

rug [rŭg] **32** 28

ruler [ro͞o′ lər] **76** 23

run [rŭn] **96** 6

rung [rŭng] **82** 9

runner [rŭn′ ər] **91** 23, **94** 31

runway [rŭn′ wā′] **57** 19

saddle [săd′ əl] **94** 20

safety glasses [sāf′ tē glăs′ əz] **78** 12

safety goggles [sāf′ tē gŏg′ əlz] **94** 28

safety pin [sāf′ tē pĭn′] **33** 11

Sahara Desert [sə hĕr′ ə dĕz′ ərt]
    71 51

sail [sāl] **59** 9

sailboard [sāl′ börd′] **59** 15

sailboat [sāl′ bōt′] **59** 4

sailor [sāl′ ər] **48** 14

salad bowl [săl′ əd bōl′] **29** 25

salad dressing [săl′ əd drĕs′ ĭng] **18** 12

salamander [săl′ ə măn′ dər] **65** 14

salesperson [sālz′ pür′ sən] **86** 12

salt shaker [sölt′ shā′ kər] **29** 10

sand (v) [sănd] **26** 14

sand (n) [sănd] **90** 31

sand dunes [sănd′ do͞onz′] **90** 12

sand trap [sănd′ trăp′] **95** 11

sandal [săn′ dəl] **20** 19

sandbox [sănd′ bŏks′] **87** 13

sandcastle [sănd′ kăs′ əl] **91** 32

sandpaper [sănd′ pā′ pər] **37** 27

sandwich [sănd′ wĭch] **16** 16

sanitation worker
    [săn ə tā′ shən wür′ kər] **49** 7

Saturn [săt′ ərn] **74** 16

saucepan [sös′ păn′] **30** 8

saucer [sö′ sər] **29** 21

sausage [sö′ sĭj] **10** 7

saw [sö] **36** 8

saxophone [săk′ sə fōn′] **98** 24

scaffolding [skăf′ əl dĭng] **82** 7

scale [skāl] **14** 7, **34** 32, **78** 4

scallop(s) [skăl′ əp(s)] **11** 35, **62** 10

scarecrow [skër′ krō′] **81** 19

scarf [skärf] **19** 19

scenery [sē′ nə rē] **99** 2

school [skōol] **76**, **77**

science lab [sī′ əns lăb′] **78**

scissors [sĭz′ərz] **101** 17

scoreboard [skör′ börd′] **93** 19

scorpion [skör′ pē ən] **63** 8

scouring pad [skowr′ ĭng păd′] **30** 11

scrape [skrāp] **26** 15

scraper [skrāp′ ər] **36** 14

screen [skrēn] **27** 19, **100** 14

screw [skrōo] **37** 42

screwdriver [skrōo′ drī′ vər] **37** 24

scrub [skrŭb] **38** 2

scuba tank [skōo′ bə tăngk′] **91** 37

sea gull [sē′ gŭl′] **64** 4

sea horse [sē′ hörs′] **65** 1

Sea of Japan [sē′ əv jə păn′] **70** 36

Sea of Okhotsk [sē′əv ō kŏtsk′]
70 35

seafood [sē′ fōod′] **10**

seal [sēl] **68** 12

seam [sēm] **101** 10

seas [sēz] **70**

seat [sēt] **52** 16, **54** 2

seat belt [sēt′ bĕlt] **50** 23

second baseman [sĕk′ ənd bās′ mən]
93 7

secretary [sĕk′ rə tër′ ē] **83** 11

section [sĕk′ shən] **8** 8a, **79** 15

security [sə kyōor′ ə tē] **56**

security guard [sə kyōor′ ə tē gärd′]
56 9, **86** 14

sedan [sə dăn′] **51**

seed [sēd] **8** 8c

seesaw [sē′ sö′] **87** 18

serve [sürv] **17** 3, **96** 2

service area [sür′ vəs ër′ ē ə] **53** 11

sevice court [sür′ vəs kört′] **95** 1

service line [sür′ vəs līn′] **95** 3

set (the table) [sĕt′ dhə tā′ bəl] **17** 8

sewing [sō′ ĭng] **101**

sewing machine [sō′ ĭng mə shēn′]
101 1

shade [shād] **33** 1

shaft [shăft] **80** 10

shampoo [shăm pōo′] **34** 8

shank [shănk] **37** 43b

shark [shärk] **65** 5

shaving cream [shā′ vĭng krēm′] **23** 22

sheep [shēp] **67** 25, **81** 10

sheet [shēt] **32** 19

sheet music [shēt′ myōo′ zĭk] **98** 2

shelf [shĕlf] **14** 6, **47** 26

shell [shĕl] **48** 27, **62** 1a, **65** 18a,
90 40

shellfish [shĕl′ fĭsh′] **11**

shepherd [shĕp′ ərd] **69** 28

shingle [shĭng′ gəl] **82** 2

ship [shĭp] **58** 9

shirt [shürt] **21** 46

shock absorbers [shŏk′ əb zör′ bərz]
52 31

shoe [shōo] **21** 49

shoelace [shōo′ lās′] **20** 7

shoot [shōot] **97** 16

shop worker [shŏp′ wür′ kər] **85** 12

shopping bag [shŏp′ ĭng băg′] **20** 18

shopping basket [shŏp′ ĭng băs′ kət]
14 8

shopping cart [shŏp′ ĭng kärt′] **15** 19

short [shört] **24** 1

short sleeve [shört′ slēv′] **20** 21

shorts [shörts] **20** 14

shortstop [shört′ stŏp′] **93** 5

shoulder [shōl′ dər] **4** 5, **53** 22

(shoulder) bag [shōl′ dər băg′] **21** 35

shovel (n) [shŭv′ əl] **27** 31, **82** 15,
90 17

shovel (v) [shŭv′ əl] **26** 13

shower cap [show′ ər kăp′] **34** 3

shower curtain [show′ ər kür′ tən] **34** 5

shower head [show′ ər hĕd′] **34** 4

shrimp [shrĭmp] **11** 31, **62** 8

shutter [shŭt′ ər] **27** 8

shuttle car [shŭt′ əl kär′] **80** 8

side [sīd] **79** 10

side mirror [sīd′ mïr′ ər] **50** 2

sideburn [sīd′ bürn′] **4** 33

sidewalk [sīd′ wök′] **45** 25

Sierra Madre [sē ër′ ə mŏ′ drē] **71** 42

silo [sī′ lō] **81** 4

silverware [sĭl′ vər wër′] **29** 22

simple animals [sĭm′ pəl ăn′ ə məlz] **62**

singer [sĭng′ ər] **99** 24

sink [sĭngk] **34** 19

sister [sĭs′ tər] **3** 10

sister-in-law [sĭs′ tər ən lö′] **3** 8

six-pack [sĭks′ păk′] **13** 13

skate (n) [skāt] **94** 26

skate (v) [skāt] **97** 9

skein [skān] **101** 24

ski [skē] **95** 17

ski boot [skē′ bōot′] **95** 15

ski cap [skē′ kăp′] **19** 16

ski lift [skē′ lĭft′] **95** 18

ski slope [skē′ slōp′] **95**

skier [skē′ ər] **94** 35

skin [skĭn] **9** 37b

skirt [skürt] **21** 36

skis [skēz] **94** 33

skunk [skŭngk] **68** 8

slacks [slăks] **20** 4

sleeping bag [slē′ pĭng băg′] **89** 26

sleepwear [slēp′ wër′] **22**

slice (n) [slīs] **13** 21

slice (v) [slīs] **31** 10

slide [slīd] **78** 31, **87** 12

slide projector [slīd′ prə jĕk′ tər]
100 13

slides [slīdz] **100** 12

sling [slĭng] **39** 3

slippers [slĭp′ərz] **22** 18

slug [slŭg] **62** 4

small [smöl] **24** 7

smoke [smōk] **42** 15

smoke detector [smōk′ də tĕk′ tər]
33 15

smokestack [smōk′ stăk′] **58** 18,
80 22

snacks [snăks] **14** 18

snail [snāl] **62** 1

snake [snāk] **65** 9

snap [snăp] **101** 13

sneakers [snē′ kərz] **20** 11

snorkel [snör′ kəl] **91** 34

snow plow [snō′ plow′] **49** 5

snowy [snō′ e] **25** 3

soap [sōp] **34** 15

soap dish [sōp′ dĭsh′] **34** 6

soccer [sŏk′ ər] **92**

soccer ball [sŏk′ ər böl′] **92** 26

socks [sŏks] **22** 17

sofa [sō/fə] **28** 25

soft drink [söft/drĭngk/] **16** 11

softball [söft/böl/] **92, 92** 10

solar collector [sō/lər kə lĕk/tər] **80** 17

solar eclipse [sō/lər ĭ klĭps/] **74** 10

solar system [sō/lər sĭs/təm] **74**

soldier [sōl/jər] **48** 16

sole [sōl] **20** 6

solid [sŏl/əd] **24** 20

solid figures [sŏl/əd fĭg/yərz] **79**

son [sŭn] **3** 16

Sony Walkman [sō/nē wök/mən] **100** 30

sore throat [sör/thrōt/] **40** 12

south [sowth] **71** 72

South America [sowth/ə mër/ə kə] **70** 2

South Atlantic [sowth/ăt lăn/tək] **70** 12

South Carolina [sowth/kăr ə lī/nə] **73** 40

South China Sea [sowth/chi/nə sē/] **70** 39

South Dakota [sowth/də kō/tə] **73** 41

South Pacific [sowth pə sĭf/ək] **70** 10

space probe [spās/prōb] **75** 4

space program [spās/prō/grăm] **75**

space shuttle [spās/shŭt/əl] **75** 14

space station [spās/stā/shən] **75** 1

space suit [spās/sōot/] **75** 6

spacecraft [spās/krăft/] **75**

spaghetti [spə gĕt/ē] **18** 10

spaniel [spăn/yəl] **69** 24

spare ribs [spër/rĭbz/] **10** 10

spare tire [spër/tīr/] **51** 39

sparrow [spăr/ō] **64** 10

spatula [spăch/ə lə] **27** 21

speaker [spē/kər] **28** 21, **100** 24

speed limit sign [spēd/lĭm ət sīn/] **53** 8

speedometer [spə dŏm/ə tər] **50** 10

spider [spī/dər] **63** 16

spinach [spĭn/əch] **6** 8

spinal cord [spī/nəl körd/] **5** 58

spiral notebook [spī/rəl nōt/bŏok] **76** 15

split [splĭt] **11** 17

split end [splĭt/ĕnd/] **93** 24

spoke [spōk] **52** 26

sponge [spŭnj] **34** 7

(sponge) mop [spŭnj/mŏp/] **35** 6

(spool of) thread [spōol/əv thrĕd/] **101** 2

spoon [spōon] **29** 8

sports car [spörts/kär/] **53** 17

sports [spörts] **92-97**

spotlight [spŏt/līt/] **99** 4

sprain [sprān] **40** 13

spray can [sprā/kăn/] **13** 24

spray starch [sprā/stärch/] **35** 21

spread [sprĕd] **17** 11

Spring [sprĭng] **26**

sprinkler [sprĭng/klər] **27** 13, **87** 14

sprocket [sprŏk/ət] **52** 20

square [skwër] **79** 9

squid [skwĭd] **62** 5

squirrel [skwür/əl] **66** 10

stage [stāj] **99** 5

staircase [stër/kās] **28** 12

stake [stāk] **89** 30

stamp [stămp] **46** 10

stands [stăndz] **93** 10

staple remover [stāp/əl rə moo/vər] **83** 29

stapler [stāp/lər] **83** 27

star [stär] **74** 4

starfish [stär/fĭsh/] **62** 7

starting gate [stär/tĭng gāt/] **95** 20

station [stā/shən] **55** 18

station wagon [stā/shən wăg/ən] **50**

steak [stāk] **10** 5, **11** 29, **18** 21

steam [stēm] **31** 12

steamer [stēm/ər] **30** 3

steering wheel [stür/ĭng wēl/] **50** 8

stem [stĕm] **8** 2a, **60** 1a

step [stĕp] **28** 13

stepladder [stĕp/lăd/ər] **35** 1

stereo cassette player [stĕr/ē ō kə sĕt plā/ər] **100** 25

stereo system [stĕr/ē ō sīs/təm] **28** 20

stern [stürn] **58** 11

stethoscope [stĕth/ə skōp/] **39** 9

stewing meat [stoo/ĭng mēt] **10** 4

stick [stĭk] **12** 5

stick shift [stĭk/shĭft/] **50** 24

sting [stĭng] **63** 8a

stingray [stĭng/rā/] **65** 6

stir [stür] **31** 1

stitch [stĭch] **101** 19

stitches [stĭch/əz] **39** 21

stockings [stŏk/ĭngz] **22** 6

stomach [stŭm/ək] **5** 66

stomachache [stŭm/ək āk/] **40** 7

stool [stōol] **78** 34

stopper [stŏp/ər] **34** 10, **78** 10

stork [störk] **64** 30

stove [stōv] **30** 30

straight line [strāt/līn/] **79** 1

(strand of) beads [strănd/əv bēdz/] **23** 7

strap [străp] **54** 8

straw [strö] **16** 10

strawberry [strö/bër/ē] **8** 15

strawberry shortcake [strö/bër ē shört/kāk] **18** 26

stream [strēm] **88** 6

street [strēt] **45** 31

street cleaner [strēt/klē/nər] **49** 1

street sign [strēt/sīn/] **44** 8

streetcar [strēt/kär/] **55** 30

streetlight [strēt/līt/] **45** 29

stretch [strĕch] **95** 19

stretch bandage [strĕch/băn/dĭj] **40** 13a

stretcher [strĕch/ər] **39** 12

stretchie [strĕch/ē] **33** 19

string [strĭng] **46** 20, **98** 10a

string bean(s) [strĭng/bēn(z)/] **6** 15

strings [strĭngz] **98**

striped [strīpt] **24** 17

stroller [strō/lər] **33** 14

student [stōo/dənt] **76** 19

stuffed animal [stŭft/ăn ə məl] **33** 27

subject [sŭb/jəkt] **47** 10

submarine [sŭb/mə rēn/] **48** 7

subway [sŭb/wā/] **54**

subway station [sŭb/wā stā/shən] **44** 16

sugar (packet) [shŏog/ər păk/ət] **16** 13

sugar bowl [shŏog/ər bōl/] **29** 23

sugarcane [shŏog/ər kān/] **60** 20

suitcase [sōot/kās/] **56** 7

Summer [sŭm/ər] **26**

sun [sŭn] **74** 7, **80** 3

sunbather [sŭn′ bā′ dhər] **90** 19

sundae [sŭn′ dē] **18** 23

sunflower [sŭn′ flŏw′ ər] **60** 19

sunglasses [sŭn′ glăs′ əz] **90** 14

sunny [sŭn′ ē] **25** 4

(sunnyside-up) egg
  [sŭn′ ē sīd ŭp′ ĕg′] **18** 32

sunroof [sŭn′ rōof′] **51** 44

suntan lotion [sŭn′ tăn lō′ shən] **91** 39

supermarket [sōo′ pər mär′ kət] **14**

surf [sürf] **97** 12

surfboard [sürf′ börd′] **91** 25

surgery [sür′ jə rē] **41** 2

suspect [sŭs′ pĕkt] **43** 3

swan [swŏn] **64** 28

sweatband [swĕt′ bănd′] **20** 12

sweater [swĕt′ ər] **19** 7, **19** 13, **19** 23

sweatpants [swĕt′ pănts′] **20** 10

sweatshirt [swĕt′ shürt′] **20** 8

sweep [swēp] **38** 7

swimmer [swĭm′ ər] **91** 28

swing [swĭng] **33** 24

swings [swĭngz] **87** 16

switch [swĭch] **37** 43c

switchboard [swĭch′ börd′] **83** 3

switchboard operator
  [swĭch′ börd ŏp′ ə rā tər] **83** 1

swordfish [sörd′ fĭsh′] **65** 3

synthesizer [sĭn′ thə sī′ zər] **99** 21

syringe [sə rĭnj′] **39** 27

syrup [sĭr′ əp] **18** 6

T-shirt [tē′ shürt′] **21** 29

table [tā′ bəl] **29** 7

tablecloth [tā′ bəl klöth′] **29** 16

tablet [tăb′ lət] **41** 6

taco [tŏ′ kō] **18** 24

tadpole [tăd′ pōl′] **65** 16

tail [tāl] **57** 10, **65** 3a, **66** 3a

taillight [tāl′ līt′] **50** 31

tailor [tā′ lər] **84** 6

take [tāk] **17** 10

takeoff [tāk′ ŏf′] **57**

Takla Makan Desert
  [tŏk′ lə mə kŏn′ dĕz′ ərt] **71** 53

tambourine [tăm′ bə rēn′] **98** 17

tank [tăngk] **48** 10

tank top [tăngk′ tŏp′] **20** 13

tanker [tăngk′ ər] **58** 15

tap [tăp] **16** 20

tape [tāp] **46** 22

tape measure [tāp′ mĕzh′ ər] **36** 21,
  101 15

taxi [tăk′ sē] **55**

taxi stand [tăk′ sē stănd′] **55** 28

taxicab [tăk′ sē kăb′] **55** 27

tea [tē] **16** 15

teacher [tē′ chər] **76** 4

teakettle [tē′ kĕt′ əl] **30** 28

team sports [tēm′ spörts′] **92**

teapot [tē′ pŏt′] **29** 19

tear [tër] **77** 9

teddy bear [tĕd′ ē bër′] **33** 3

tee [tē] **95** 13

telephone [tĕl′ ə fōn′] **83** 15

telescope [tĕl′ ə skōp′] **74** 22

television [tĕl′ ə vĭzh′ ən] **28** 18, **100** 5

teller [tĕl′ ər] **86** 15

temperature [tĕm′ pər ə chər] **25** 6

Tennessee [tĕn′ ə sē′] **73** 42

tennis [tĕn′ əs] **94**

tennis ball [tĕn′ əs böl′] **94** 1

tennis court [tĕn′ əs kört′] **95**

tent [tĕnt] **89** 24

tentacle [tĕn′ tə kəl] **62** 12a

terminal [türm′ ə nəl] **51** 55, **58** 29

terminal building [türm′ ə nəl bĭl′ dĭng]
  57 16

termite [tür′ mīt] **63** 11

terrier [tĕr′ ē ər] **69** 25

test tube [tĕst′ tōob′] **78** 9

Texas [tĕk′ səs] **73** 43

textbook [tĕkst′ bŏok′] **76** 26

theater [thē′ ə tər] **99**

thermometer
  [thər möm′ ə tər] **25** 5, **78** 22

thermos [thür′ məs] **88** 14

thigh [thī] **4** 18, **11** 19

thimble [thĭm′ bəl] **101** 21

third (1/3) [thürd] **79** 32

third baseman [thürd′ bās′ mən] **93** 4

thorn [thörn] **60** 18c

thread [thrĕd] **37** 42b, **101** 2

three-piece suit [thrē′ pēs sōot] **21** 40

throat [thrōt] **5** 59

through [thrōo] **103** 1

throw [thrō] **97** 10

thumb [thŭm] **4** 24

thumbtack [thŭm′ tăk′] **76** 25

ticket [tĭk′ ət] **55** 16, **56** 4

ticket window [tĭk′ ət wĭn′ dō] **55** 19

tie (n) [tī] **21** 47

tie (v) [tī] **77** 12

tie clip [tī′ klĭp′] **23** 14

tie pin [tī′ pĭn′] **23** 13

tiger [tī′ gər] **68** 2

tight [tīt] **24** 3

tighten [tī′ tən] **38** 4

tight end [tīt′ ĕnd′] **93** 30

tights [tīts] **19** 14

tile [tīl] **34** 27

timer [tī′ mər] **78** 13

timetable [tīm′ tă′ bəl] **55** 20

tip [tĭp] **55** 22

tire [tīr] **50** 37, **52** 28

tissues [tĭsh′ ōoz] **32** 13

title [tī′ təl] **47** 9

to [tōo] **103** 9

toast [tōst] **18** 34

toaster [tōs′ tər] **30** 16

toe [tō] **5** 54

toenail [tō′ nāl′] **5** 56

toilet [toy′ lət] **34** 29

toilet brush [toy′ lət brŭsh′] **34** 31

toilet paper [toy′ lət pā′ pər] **34** 30

toiletries [toy′ lə trēz] **23**

token booth [tō′ kən bōoth′] **54** 13

tollbooth [tōl′ bōoth′] **53** 27

tomato(es) [tə mā′ tō(z)] **7** 19

tongs [tŏngz] **78** 29

tongue [tŭng] **4** 41

tongue depressor [tŭng′ də prĕs′ ər]
  40 12a

toolbox [tōol′ bŏks′] **36** 23

toolshed [tōol′ shĕd′] **27** 28

tooth [tōoth] **4** 42

toothache [tōoth′ āk′] **40** 9

toothbrush [tōoth′ brŭsh′] **34** 21

toothless mammals [tōoth′ ləs măm′ əlz]
  66

toothpaste [tōoth′ pāst′] **34** 16

tortoise [tör′ təs] **65** 18

tossed salad [töst′ săl′ əd] **18** 13

touch [tŭch] **77** 2

touring handlebars
    [toor' ĭng hăn' dəl bärz] **52** 12

tow truck [tō' trŭk] **49** 2

toward [törd] **103** 4

towel rack [tow' əl răk'] **34** 25

towrope [tō' rōp'] **59** 11

toy chest [toy' chĕst'] **33** 29

track [trăk] **54** 10, **94** 32

track and field [trăk' ənd fēld'] **94**

tractor [trăk' tər] **81** 15

tractor trailer [trăk' tər trā' lər] **49** 15

traffic cop [trăf' ək kŏp'] **44** 10

traffic light [trăf' ək līt'] **45** 21

trailer [trā' lər] **53** 10

train [trān] **55**

training wheels [trān' ĭng wēlz'] **52** 1

transcript [trăn' skrĭpt] **43** 15

transfer [trăns' fər] **54** 4

transformer [trăns för' mər] **80** 25

transmission towers
    [trănz mĭsh' ən tow' ərz] **80** 23

transportation [trăns' pər tā' shən] **54**

transporter [trăns' pör tər] **49** 17

trash basket [trăsh' băs' kət] **44** 15

trash can [trăsh' kăn'] **87** 11

travel agent [trăv' əl ā' jənt] **84** 4

traveler [trăv' ə lər] **56** 3

tray [trā] **16** 33

tray table [trā' tā' bəl] **56** 22

treatments [trēt' mənts] **41**

tree [trē] **61** 35

trees [trēz] **60**

triangle [trī' ăng' gəl] **79** 6

tricycle [trī' sĭ kəl] **52** 6

trigger [trĭg' ər] **48** 22

tripod [trī' pod] **100** 9

trim [trĭm] **26** 8

trombone [trŏm bōn'] **98** 23

trough [tröf] **81** 25

trout [trowt] **65** 2

trowel [trow' əl] **27** 27

truck [trŭk] **49**, **53** 25

truck driver [trŭk' drī' vər] **49** 16

trumpet [trŭm' pət] **98** 25

trunk [trŭngk] **51** 40, **61** 35b, **66** 17a

tub [tŭb] **12** 6

tuba [too' bə] **98** 27

tube [toob] **13** 15, **91** 29

tugboat [tŭg' bōt'] **58** 13

tulip [too' ləp] **60** 1

turkey [tür' kē] **10** 23, **64** 20

turnip [tür' nəp] **7** 34

turn signal lever [türn' sĭg nəl lĕ' vər]
    50 11

turn signal lights [türn' sĭg nəl līts']
    51 50

turnstile [türn' stīl'] **54** 12

turntable [türn' tā' bəl] **100** 18

turtle [tür' təl] **65** 12

(turtleneck) sweater
    [tür' təl nĕk swĕ' tər] **19** 13

tusk [tŭsk] **66** 17b

TV antenna [tē' vē ăn tĕn' ə] **27** 3

tweezers [twē' zərz] **78** 32

twig [twĭg] **61** 33a

(two-door) sedan [too' dör sə dăn'] **51**

type [tīp] **77** 10

typewriter [tīp' rī' tər] **83** 10

typing chair [tī' pĭng chër'] **83** 17

typist [tī' pəst] **83** 6

U.S. mailbox [yoo' ĕs māl' bŏks] **46** 6

U.S. Postal System
    [yoo' ĕs pōs' təl sĭs təm] **46**

ukulele [yoo' kə lā' lē] **98** 3

umbrella [ŭm brĕl' ə] **20** 24

umpire [ŭm' pīr] **92** 1, **93** 17

uncle [ŭng' kəl] **3** 3

under [ŭn' dər] **102** 8

underpants [ŭn' dər pănts'] **22** 3

undershirt [ŭn' dər shürt'] **22** 1

underwear [ŭn' dər wër'] **22**

uniform [yoo' nə förm'] **21** 45, **92** 9

United States of America
    [yoo nī' təd stāts' əv əmër' ə kə] **72**

universe [yoo' nə vürs'] **74**

up [ŭp] **103** 11

upper arm [ŭp' ər ärm'] **4** 7

Urals [yoor' əlz] **71** 46

uranium rods [yoo rā' nē əm rŏdz']
    80 15

Uranus [yoor' ə nəs] **74** 17

usher [ŭsh' ər] **99** 16

Utah [yoo' tö] **73** 44

utility pole [yoo tĭl' ə tē pōl'] **80** 26

utility room [yoo tĭl' ə tē room'] **35**

(V-neck) sweater [vē' nĕk swĕt' ər]
    19 23

vacuum [văk' yoom] **38** 14

vacuum cleaner [văk' yoom klē' nər]
    35 16

valve [vălv] **52** 27

van [văn] **53** 26

vase [vās] **28** 6

VCR (videocassette recorder)
    [vē' sē är']/
    [vĭd' ē ō kə sĕt' rə kör' dər] **100** 4

vegetables [vĕj' tə bəlz] **6**

vehicles and equipment
    [vē' ə kəlz ənd ə kwĭp' mənt] **48**

vein [vān] **5** 68

vendor [vĕn' dər] **87** 3

vent [vĕnt] **50** 21

Venus [vē' nəs] **74** 12

verbs [vürbz] **17**, **26**, **31**, **38**, **77**, **96**

Vermont [vür mŏnt'] **73** 45

vest [vĕst] **21** 39

video [vĭd' ē ō] **100**

video camera [vĭd' ē ō kăm' ə rə]
    100 1

videocassette (tape)
    [vĭd' ē ō kə sĕt' tāp'] **100** 3

vine [vīn] **61** 42

viola [vē ōl' ə] **98** 8

violet [vī' ə lət] **60** 16

violin [vī ə lĭn'] **98** 7

Virginia [vər jĭn' yə] **73** 46

vise [vīs] **37** 36

visor [vīz' ər] **50** 5

volleyball [vŏl' ē böl'] **92**, **92** 22

waders [wā' dərz] **88** 10

waist [wāst] **4** 13

waiter [wā tər] **16** 5

waitress [wā' trəs] **16** 2

walk [wök] **77** 8

walker [wök' ər] **33** 23

wall [wöl] **28** 3

wall unit [wöl' yoo' nət] **28** 19

wall-to-wall carpeting
    [wöl' tə wöl kär' pə tĭng] **28** 15

wallet [wöl' ət] **20** 9

walnut(s) [wöl' nət(s)] **9** 29

walrus [wöl' rŭs] **68** 11

warm [wörm] **25** 8

wash [wŏsh] **38** 16

washcloth [wŏsh′klŏth′] **34** 22

washer [wŏsh′ər] **37** 40

washing machine
[wŏsh′ĭng mə shēn′] **35** 30

Washington [wŏsh′ĭng tən] **73** 47

wasp [wŏsp] **63** 20

wastepaper basket
[wāst′pā pər băs′kət] **34** 13

watch [wŏch] **23** 10

watchband [wŏch′bănd′] **23** 11

water (*n*) [wŏt′ər] **42** 16, **91** 30

water (*v*) [wŏt′ər] **26** 5

water fountain [wŏt′ər fown′tən]
87 19

water glass [wŏt′ər glăs′] **29** 6

waterfall [wŏt′ər föl] **80** 11, **89** 18

water-skier [wŏt′ər skē′ər] **59** 10

watercress [wŏt′ər krĕs′] **6** 5

watering can [wŏt′ər ĭng kăn′] **27** 16

watermelon [wŏt′ər mĕl′ ən] **9** 26

wave [wāv] **91** 24

weapon [wĕp′ənz] **48**

weather [wĕdh′ər] **25**

weather forecaster
[wĕdh′ər för′ kăst ər] **86** 1

weather satellite [wĕdh′ər săt′ ə līt]
75 3

weaving [wē′ vĭng] **101** 30

web [wĕb] **63** 15

wedding ring [wĕd′ĭng rĭng′] **23** 4

weights [wāts] **78** 5

west [wĕst] **71** 74

West Virginia [wĕst′ vər jĭn′ yə] **73** 48

wet [wĕt] **25** 15

wet suit [wĕt′ sōot′] **91** 38

whale [wāl] **68** 9

wheat [wēt] **60** 22

wheat farm [wēt′ färm′] **81**

(wheat) field [wēt′ fēld′] **81** 16

wheel [wēl] **52** 4

wheelbarrow [wēl′ băr′ ō] **27** 32,
82 23

wheelchair [wēl′ chër′] **39** 2

whistle [wĭs′ əl] **90** 5

whole [hōl] **11** 27, **79** 29

whole (chicken) [hōl′ chĭk′ ən] **11** 16

width [wĭdth] **79** 35

wife [wīf] **2** 4

willow [wĭl′ ō] **61** 31

wind [wĭnd] **80** 4

windbreaker [wĭnd′ brā′ kər] **19** 5

windlass [wĭnd′ ləs] **58** 23

windmill [wĭnd′ mĭl′] **80** 19

window [wĭn′ dō] **27** 7, **46** 15

window cleaner [wĭn′ dō klē′ nər]
35 10

windpipe [wĭnd′ pīp′] **5** 60

windshield [wĭnd′ shēld′] **51** 45

windshield wiper [wĭnd′ shēld wī′ pər]
50 6

windsurfer [wĭnd′ sür′ fər] **59** 14

windy [wĭn′ dē] **25** 13

wine [wīn] **16** 19

wine glass [wīn′ glăs′] **29** 5

wing [wĭng] **11** 22, **57** 9, **63** 4a,
64 1a

Winter [wĭn′ tər] **26**

wipe [wīp] **38** 5

wire [wīr] **37** 35

wire mesh screen [wīr′ mĕsh skrēn′]
78 6

Wisconsin [wĭs kŏn′ sən] **73** 49

witness [wĭt′ nəs] **43** 13

witness stand [wĭt′ nəs stănd′] **43** 18

wolf [wŏolf] **69** 29

woman [wŏom′ ən] **2** 1

wood [wŏod] **36** 4

wood plane [wŏod′ plān′] **37** 32

woodpecker [wŏod′ pĕk′ ər] **64** 17

woods [wŏodz] **89** 32

woodwinds [wŏod′ wĭndz′] **98**

wool [wŏol] **101** 23

word processor [würd′ prŏ′ sĕs ər]
83 7

work gloves [würk′ glŭvz′] **27** 26

workbench [würk′ bĕnch′] **36** 22

workshop [würk′ shŏp′] **36**

world [würld] **70**

worm [würm] **62** 11

wrench [rĕnch] **36** 10

wrist [rĭst] **4** 21

write [rīt] **77** 7

writer [rī′ tər] **86** 7

Wyoming [wī ō′ mĭng] **73** 50

X ray [ĕks′ rā′] **39** 1

X ray screener [ĕks′ rā skrē′ nər] **56** 11

xylophone [zī′ lə fōn′] **98** 31

yam [yăm] **7** 24

Yangtze River [yăng′ sē rĭv′ ər] **71** 69

yarn [yärn] **101** 31

Yellow Sea [yĕl′ ō sē′] **70** 37

Yenisey River [yĕn′ ə sā′ rĭv′ ər]
71 65

Yukon River [yōo′ kŏn rĭv′ ər] **71** 56

zebra [zē′ brə] **66** 18

zinnia [zĭn′ ē ə] **60** 13

zip code [zĭp′ kōd′] **46** 12

zipper [zĭp′ ər] **101** 16

zoo [zōo] **87** 1

zucchini [zōo kē′ nē] **7** 27

a (la cancha de golf) **103** 9
a (la colina) **103** 11
a cuadros **24** 18
a través de (el faro) **103** 1
abajo (del gato blanco) **102** 3
abarrotes **15** 24
abdomen **4** 14
abedul **61** 32
abeja **63** 19
abierto **24** 15
abogado defensor **43** 22
abordaje **56**
abrelatas **30** 4
abrigo **19** 24, **42** 13
abrigo de invierno **19** 8
abrir **31** 3
abuela **3** 1
abuelo **3** 2
abuelos **2** 10
acampando **89**
accesorios **35** 17
acebo **61** 37
aceitar **38** 12
aceite de motor **80** 33
acelerador **50** 27
acera **45** 25
acolchado (sustantivo) **101** 32
acomodador **99** 16
acoplado **49** 18
acordeón **98** 28
actividades al aire libre **88, 89**
actor **99** 19
actriz **99** 20
acumulador **51** 54
acusado **43** 23
aderezo **18** 12
Africa **70** 4
agalla **65** 3c
agarrar **17** 10, **96** 4
agarradera **30** 34, **54** 8
agente de bienes raíces **85** 5
agente de viajes **84** 4
agrifolio **61** 37
agua **42** 16, **91** 30
aguacate **9** 33
aguantar **17** 12
aguaviva **62** 12

aguijón **63** 8a
el águila **64** 5
aguja **39** 26, **61** 34a, **101** 18
aguja de cartucho **100** 19
aguja de gancho **101** 29
aguja de tejer **101** 25
agujeta **20** 7
aire acondicionado **32** 11
ajo **7** 25
ajolote **65** 16
al otro lado de (el agua) **103** 6
ala **11** 22, **57** 9, **63** 4a, **64** 1a
ala extrema **93** 24, **93** 30
Alabama **72** 1
alacena de loza **29** 2
alacrán **63** 8
álamo **61** 30
Alaska **72** 2
albaricoque **9** 25
albóndigas **18** 11
alcachofa **6** 11
alcancía de cuota **54** 5
alcantarilla **45** 32
alce **67** 35
alcohol **39** 22
aleta **65** 3b
aletas **91** 36
alfiler **101** 20
alfiler de corbata **23** 13
alfiletero **101** 3
alfombra **32** 28, **50** 22
alfombra (de baño) **34** 12
alfombrado (de pared a pared) **28** 15
algodón **39** 23
algodoncito **33** 10
alijadora **36** 14
alicate **36** 19
alimentos congelados **14** 2
alimentos de mar Mariscos **11** C
alimentos preparados comunes **18**
almeja(s) **11** 32, **62** 3
almendra(s) **9** 31
almíbar **18** 6
almidón en lata rociadora **35** 21
almohada **32** 16
Alpes **71** 44
alpinismo **89**

alrededor de (el faro) **103** 2
alta presión sanguínea **40** 10
alto **24** 11
altoparlante **76** 3, **100** 24
altura **79** 34
alunizaje **75** B
ama de llaves **85** 8
amarrar **77** 12
Amazonas **71** 59
ambulancia **42** 6
ametralladora **48** 25
amortiguadores **52** 31
amplificador de microfilm **47** 14
anacardo(s) **9** 27
ancho **79** 35
el ancla **58** 24
anclaje **59** 19
andadera **33** 23
anador **33** 23
Andes **71** 43
anfibios y reptiles **65** B
anguila **65** 4
ángulo agudo **79** 8
ángulo obtuso **79** 5
ángulo recto **79** 23
anillo(s) **23** 2, **74** 16a
anillo de boda **23** 4
anillo de compromiso **23** 3
animal de peluche **33** 27
Animales sencillos **62**
anotador **43** 14
Antártica **70** 7
Antártico **70** 14
antebrazo **4** 9
antena **51** 46, **62** 1b
antena de televisión **27** 3
anteojos **21** 44
anular **4** 27
anzar **97** 10
apagador **32** 25
aparador **29** 29
aparejo **89** 22
apartamentos **45** 23
ápice **79** 21
apio **6** 10
apretado **24** 3
apretar **38** 4

arándano agrios **8** 13

arándano azules **8** 14

araña **63** 16

arandela **37** 40

árbitro **92** 1, **93** 17, **93** 22, **94** 16

árbol **61** 35

árbol frutal **81** 2

árboles **61**

arbustos **61** 41

arce **61** 38

archivero **83** 21

archivista **83** 23

archivo **83** 22

arco **79** 16, **98** 7a

arcón **15** 16

ardilla **66** 10

ardillita **66** 6

el área de carga **57** 12

área de juego **87** 15

área de picnic **88**

área de servicios **53** 11

área habitacional **75** 11

área postal **46** 12

área verde **95** 10

área verde y plana **95** 12

arena **91** 31

arenoso **71** 55

arete de broche **23** 16

arete de presión **23** 15

aretes **23** 1

Arizona **72** 3

Arkansas **72** 4

arma **43** 7

Armada **48** 15

armadillo **66** 2

armario **29** 2, **76** 6

armas y munición **48** C

armazón **80** 2

aros para cortina **34** 2

arquitecto **86** 8

arreglista **99** 22

arrojar **97** 10

arroyuelo **88** 6

arroz **60** 21

arteria **5** 69

Artico **70** 8

artículos de tocador y maquillaje **23** B

artículos del hogar **15** 15

el, la artista **86** 3

asado **10** 3, **18** 14

asador **30** 33

asar **31** 13

ascensor **45** 17

ascensor de esquíes **95** 18

Asia **70** 5

asiento **16** 25, **52** 16, **54** 2

asiento deportivo **50** 16

asiento para niño **50** 33

asiento trasero **50** 32

asistente **53** 12

asoleadera **27** 5

aspiradora **35** 16

aspirar **38** 14

asta **67** 35a

asteroide **74** 20

astil **37** 43b

astronauta **75** 5

Atacama **71** 50

atajador derecho **93** 29

atajador izquierdo **93** 25

Atlántico del norte **70** 11

Atlántico del sur **70** 12

atlas **47** 20

atletismo **94**

atrás **23** 19

audífonos **100** 29, **83** 2

audio **100** D

auditorio **99** 15

auriculares **83** 2

Australia **70** 6

autobús **54** A, **53** 20

autor **47** 8

avellana(s) **9** 30

aventar **97** 10

Aves **64**

aves de corral **11** B

el avestruz **64** 12

aviador **48** 20

avión de caza **48** 1

avión de motor **57** 7

aviones **57**

avispa **63** 20

axila **4** 10

ayudante **39** 8, **53** 12

ayudante de camarero **16** 3

azafrán croco **60** 9

azúcar (paquetito de) **16** 13

azucarera **29** 23

azucena **60** 3

azulejo **34** 27

babero **33** 20

babosa **62** 4

baboso **62** 4

Bahía Baffin **70** 16

Bahía de Bengala **70** 32

Bahía del Hudson **70** 18

el bailarín **99** 3

la bailarina **99** 3

bajada **95** C

bajo **24** 12, **98** 10, **99** 23

bajón **98** 14

bala **48** 26

balcón **27** 6, **99** 14

balde **90** 16

ballena **68** 9

el ballet **99** A

balón **92** 21, **92** 26

baloncesto **92**

balsa **89** 16

banca **44** 14, **87** 10

banco **43** 16, **78** 34, **93** 13

banda **15** 23, **20** 12, **56** 12

banda (del ventilador) **51** 53

bandeja **16** 33, **37** 28

bandeja de asar **30** 17

bandera **76** 1, **95** 9

banderín **95** 9

bañera **34** 11

banjo **98** 5

el, la bañista **90** 19

el baño **34**

banqueta **45** 25

baqueta **43** 8

bar **16** B, **16** 24

barba **4** 39

barbilla **4** 3

barcaza **58** 12

barco de carga **58** 9

barco de guerra **48** 5

barco tanque **58** 15

barquillo **18** 36

barquillo de nieve **18** 36

barra de balance **94** 24

barra de pan **12** 7

barra **13** 18, **16** 24

barranca **89** 21

barredora **49** 1

barrer **38** 7

barrita **12** 5

báscula **34** 32

base **79** 7, **93** 6, **93** 15

basinica **33** 33

bastilla **101** 12

basurero **34** 13, **35** 31, **44** 15, **87** 11

bata **43** 11

bata (de baño) **22** 20

bata de noche **22** 21

bate **92** 5

batea **12** 6

bateador **92** 7, **93** 14

batería **51** 54

baterista **99** 27

batir **31** 8

batuta **99** 9

baúl **51** 40

baúl de juguetes **33** 29

bayas **8**

bayoneta **48** 24

bebé **2** 5

bebedero **81** 25, **87** 19

beber **17** 2

bebidas **14** 14

becerro **67** 31

béisbol **92**

bellota **61** 33b

berenjena **7** 21

berro **6** 5

betabel(es) **7** 33

biberón **33** 17

la biblioteca pública **47**

bibliotecaria **47** 23

bicicleta(s) **52** , **52** 15

bicicleta de hombre **52** 11

bicicleta de mujer **52** 3

bicicleta para campo **52** 8

biftec **10** 5

bigote **4** 40

billete(s) **13** 25

billete de transbordo **54** 4

billetera **20** 9

binoculares **90** 7

bisonte **67** 19

bisquet **18** 27

bisté **10** 5, **11** 29, **18** 21

blanqueador **35** 26

block (de papel) **83** 26

block para mensajes **83** 25

bloques **33** 32

blusa **21** 34

boca **4** 2, **62** 13a

bocadillos **15** 18

bocina **28** 21, **50** 12, **52** 5, **76** 3, **100** 24

bodega **58** 8

boina **19** 22

bola **5** 52

bola de boliche **94** 6

bola de frontón **94** 12

bola de frontón con raqueta **94** 30

bola de golf **94** 7

bola de ping-pong **94** 19

bola de tenis **94** 1

bolardo **58** 26

boleto **54** 4, **55** 16, **56** 4

boliche **94**

bolígrafo **76** 22

bolillos de tambor **98** 19a

bolla **59** 19

bolo **94** 5

bolos **94**

bolsa **12** 8, **15** 25, **21** 41, **66** 3c

bolsa de compras **20** 18

bolsa de correo **46** 4

bolsa de golf **95** 7

bolsa de hielo **41** 4

bolsa para dormir **89** 26

bolsillo **21** 41

bolso **21** 35, **20** 23

bolso de mano **56** 2

bomba de agua para incendios **42** 9

bomba de aire **53** 13

bomba de gasolina **53** 14

bomba **35** 14, **48** 3

bombardero **48** 2

bombero **42** 10

bombilla **35** 22

bongos **98** 22

bordado **101** 27

borde **53** 22

borrador **76** 11, **76** 21

borrar **77** 3

borrego **67** 24

borregos **81** 10

bosques **89** 32

bota de esquiar **95** 15

botalón **59** 7

botar **97** 11

botas **19** 21, **21** 32, **88** 10

botas de excursionismo **19** 9

botas de lluvia **19** 25

botavara **59** 7

bote **59** 18

bote de paseo **59** 16

bote de pesca **58** 1

bote de remo **59** 23

bote de vela **59** 4

bote salvavidas **58** 19, **90** 10

botecito **59** 18

botella **12** 3

(botella de) licor **16** 22

botiquín **34** 14

botón **20** 3, **60** 18a, **101** 9

botón de oro **60** 17

boxeo **94**

boya **58** 16

brazalete **23** 9

brazo **4** 6, **100** 20

brillo **30** 11

brincar **96** 8

brocha **37** 30, **76** 18

broche **23** 17

broche de corbata **23** 14

broche de presión **101** 13

brocoli **6** 2

bufanda **19** 19

búho **64** 6

bulbo **60** 8a

(bulto de) paja **81** 13

buque **58** 27

buró **32** 9

burro **67** 23

bustillo **22** 9

buzón **46** 1

buzón de los Estados Unidos **46** 6
cabalgar **97** 13
caballista **87** 6
caballito de San Pedro **63** 4
caballitos **87** 5
caballo **67** 21
caballo de mar **65** 1
caballos **81** 23
cabecera **32** 14
cabello **4** 30
cabeza **4** C, **37** 42a
(cabeza de) coliflor **6** 1
cabina **56** 19
cabina de mando **56** 13
cable **52** 23
cable eléctrico **37** 35
cacahuete(s) **9** 28
cacerola **30** 8, **30** 14, **37** 28
cachar **96** 4
cácher **92** 2, **93** 16
cachete **4** 35
cachorro **69** 27
cachucha **21** 43
cactus **61** 40
cadena **23** 5, **52** 18
cadera **4** 16
caer **96** 7
café **18** 35
cafetera **29** 18, **30** 31
caída de agua **80** 11
caja **13** 12, **15** 21, **58** 7
caja de fusibles **35** 5
caja de herramientas **36** 23
cajera **15** 22
cajero **15** 22, **86** 15
cajetilla **13** 16
cajón **47** 5
cajón de arena **87** 13
cajuela **51** 40
calabacita **7** 27
calabaza **7** 26
calabaza pequeña **7** 28
calamar **62** 5
calcetines **22** 17
calcetines largos **22** 16
calculadora **83** 19, **100** 34
caldero **30** 13

calefacción **80** 27
calendario **83** 9
caliente **25** 7
California **72** 5
calle **45** 31
caluroso **25** 8
calzón **22** 3
calzón largo **22** 7
calzoncillo **22** 3
calzoncillo boxer **22** 2
cama **32** 21
cámara **100** 8
cámara de cine **100** 15
cámara de video **100** 1
camarógrafo **86** 10
camarón **11** 31, **62** 8
cambiar (las sábanas) **38** 13
cambio de velocidades **50** 17
camello **67** 33
camilla **39** 12
caminar **77** 8
camino de harradura **87** 7
camino entarimado **90** 1
camión **49** 9, **53** 25
camión de la basura **49** 6
camión de correo **46** 5
camión de mudanza **53** 26
camión de volteo **49** 14
camionero **49** 16
camiones **49**
camioneta **49** 4, **50** C
camioneta cuatro puertas **51** E
camioneta de lonchar **49** 8
camisa **21** 46
camisa de franela **19** 3
camiseta **22** 1
camiseta manga corta **21** 29
camiseta sin mangas **20** 13
camisola **22** 9
camisón **22** 21
campista central **93** 2
campista delantero **93** 5
campista derecho **93** 3
campista izquierdo **93** 1
campo **93** 5
campo de fútbol **93** B
campo de golf **95** B

campos de juego **93**
campos y canchas de juego **95**
canal **94** 3
canal de tizas **76** 9
canalizador **37** 37
canario **64** 14
canasta **15** 16, **92** 20
canasta de compras **14** 8
canasta de día de campo **88** 13
canasto **34** 28
canasto de lavandería **35** 29
cancha **94** 13
cancha de tenis **95** A
candelero **29** 28
candil **29** 3
caneva **101** 26
cangrejo **62** 9
canguro **66** 3
canoa **59** 2
canoa de los esquimales **59** 17
cantante **99** 24
cantina **16** B
cantina rodante **49** 8
cantinero **16** 21
caña de azúcar **60** 20
caña de pesca **88** 7
cañón **48** 11, **48** 23, **88** 3
capa de agua **21** 38
el, la capataz **85** 13
capota **51** 47
cápsula **41** 5
capullo **63** 2
cara **4** 1
caracol **62** 1, **91** 40
carapacho **65** 18a
carbón **27** 23, **80** 7
cárcel **43** 1
cardenal **64** 11
careta **91** 35, **92** 15
carga **58** 10
cargar **26** 16
carne **10** A
carne, aves, y mariscos **10, 11**
carne de puerco **10** 6
carne de res **10** 1
carne molida **10** 2
carne para cocido **10** 4

carnicero **84** 13

Carolina del norte **73** 33

Carolina del sur **73** 40

carpeta **76** 14

carpintero **85** 2

carreras de caballo **94**

carreta tirada por caballos **55** 33

(carrete de) hilo **101** 2

carretera interestatal **53** 1

carretilla **27** 32

carril **54** 10, **94** 4

carril central **53** 6

carril de entrada **53** 21

carril de salida **53** 2

carril derecho **53** 7

carril izquierdo **53** 5

carrito de bebé **33** 14

carrito de compras **15** 19

carrito de equipaje **56** 6

carrito de golf **95** 8

carrito manual **87** 4

carro bombas **42** 2

carro casa **53** 16

carro de bomberos **42** 3

carro de ferrocarríl **54** 9

carro de mudanza **49** 11

carro de pasajeros **53** 15

carro deportivo **53** 17

carro para bebé **45** 27

carro tanque de bomberos **42** 2

carro tanque **49** 3

carros **50** , **51**

carta **46** 7

cartera **20** 9, **20** 23

(carterita de) cerillos **16** 28

carterita **13** 17

cartero **46** 3

cartón **12** 1

casa de campaña **89** 24

casa de energía **80** 20

casa de fuerza **80** 20

casa de granja **81** 3

casa de muñecas **33** 25

casa de rancho **27** A

casa estilo colonial **27** B

casa-remolque **53** 10

casas **27**

cascada **80** 11, **89** 18

cáscara **8** 8b, **9** 3a, **9** 37b

casco **21** 28, **42** 12, **52** 7, **92** 14

casco del bateador **92** 6

casco protector **94** 14

caseta **16** 9

caseta de cobro **53** 27

caseta de taxis **55** 28

casilla **54** 13

casquillo **48** 27

cassette **100** 26

castaña(s) **9** 32

castillo de arena **91** 32

castor **66** 12

catálogo **47** 4

catarina **63** 14

catsup **16** 4

cazuela **30** 17

cebolla(s) **7** 31

cebra **66** 18

ceja **5** 44

cello **98** 9

cenicero **16** 29

centavo **13** 27

centro **8** 2b, **79** 13, **93** 27

cepillo de baño **34** 31

cepillo de dientes **34** 21

cepillo de madera **37** 32

cepillo de pelo **32** 7

cepillo para uñas **34** 20

cerca **81** 9

cerdo **10** 6, **67** 30

cerebro·**5** 57

cerezas **9** 19 ·

cerillos **16** 28

cerrado **24** 16

cerrajero **85** 4

cerrar **77** 5

cervato **67** 27

cerveza **16** 23

cerveza de barril **20** 16

césped **27** 15

chabacano **9** 25

chaleco **21** 39

chaleco de plumas de ganso **19** 12

chaleco salvavidas **59** 1

chamarra **19** 17

chamarra de invierno **19** 8

champú **34** 8

chancletas **22** 18

chango **69** 14

chapa **43** 5

chapa de matrícula **50** 28

chapaletas **91** 36

chapulín **63** 6

chaqueta **19** 17

charola **16** 33

charola para cubitos de hielo **30** 21

chavito prieto **13** 27

cheque **15** 27

chícharo(s) **6** 17

chico **24** 7

chimenea **27** 9, **28** 8, **58** 18, **80** 22

chimpancé **69** 16

china **8** 8

chinero **29** 2

chiringa **91** 22

chivo **67** 28

chofer **49** 16, **54** 3

chopo **61** 30

chorizo **10** 7

chorrera **87** 12

chorrito **87** 14

chuletas **10** 15

chuletas de puerco **10** 9, **18** 15

chupón **33** 22

ciclista **90** 4

ciempiés **63** 22

cierre **101** 16

cigarillo **16** 31

cigarro **16** 31

cigüeña **64** 30

cilindro **79** 26

cilindro graduado **78** 25

cinta **20** 12, **46** 22, **100** 3, **100** 26

cinta de aislar **37** 34

cinta de medir **36** 21

cinta métrica **101** 15

cintas **100** 25

cintura **4** 13

cinturón **20** 16

cinturón de seguridad **50** 23

círculo **79** 11

circunferencia **79** 17

ciruela **9** 34

ciruela pasa **9** 23

cirugía **41** 2

cisne **64** 28

la ciudad **44, 45**

clarabolla **58** 21

clarinete **98** 16

claro **24** 9

clases de aviones **57** A

clavelón **60** 6

clavija **37** 43d

clavija de tierra **36** 7

clavo **37** 41

claxon **50** 12, **52** 5

cliente **15** 17

closet **32** 3

clutch **50** 25

cobertor acolchado **32** 22

cobija **32** 20

cobra **65** 11

coche **54** 9

coches **50, 51**

la cocina **30**

cocinar **17** 4

cocinar a vapor **31** 12

cocinero **16** 1

coco **8** 3

cocodrilo **65** 8

cocuyo **63** 2

código postal **46** 12

codo **4** 8

cohete **75** 13

cojín **28** 24

cojincillo de restregar **30** 11

col **6** 3

cola **57** 10, **65** 3a, **66** 3a

coladera **30** 7

colador **30** 7

colcha **32** 23

colchón **32** 17

colchón de aire **91** 26

colchón de muelles **32** 18

colchón protector **33** 5

colector solar **80** 17

coles pequeñas **6** 4

colgar **38** 6

colibrí **64** 2

colina **88** 4

collar **23** 6

collar de cuentas **23** 7

colmillo **66** 17b

colocar **17** 8

Colorado **72** 6

colorados **6** 13

colorete **23** 32

columpio **33** 24

columpios **87** 16

combate del fuego y rescate **42**

combustible diesel **80** 34

combustible para jet **80** 31

comedia musical **99** B

el comedor **29**

comer **17** 1

cometa **74** 2, **91** 22

cómoda **32** 30

compartimento de equipaje **56** 21

comprador **15** 17

compra **15** 24

compuerta trasera **51** 43

computadora **76** 8, **83** 16

computadoras **100** E

concha **62** 1a, **62** 10, **65** 18a, **91** 40

conductor **54** 3, **54** 7, **99** 8

conejo **66** 13

conexión **32** 26b

confitería **15** 18

conga **98** 20

congelado (y resbaloso) **25** 16

congelador **14** 3, **30** 20

Congo **71** 62

conmutador **83** 3

Connecticut **72** 7

cono **61** 34b, **79** 28

constelación (Osa Mayor) **74** 3

contacto **36** 6

contador **86** 18

continentes **70**

contraventana **27** 8

control remoto **28** 17

copa de vino **29** 5

copiloto **56** 16

corazón **5** 64, **8** 2b

corbata **21** 47

corcho **16** 18, **61** 35c

cordero **10** 13, **67** 25

cordilleras **71**

cordón **20** 7, **32** 26a, **46** 20, **54** 1

cordón de pesca **88** 8

cornejo **61** 28

corneta francesa **98** 26

coro **99** 18

corral **81** 8, **81** 24

corral de juego **33** 30

correa **20** 16

correa de reloj **23** 11

correcaminos **64** 32

corredor **94** 31

corredores **91** 23

correo **46** 2

correr **96** 6

corta **24** 1

corta circuitos **35** 5

corta uñas **23** 31

cortada **40** 16

cortadora de césped (grama) **27** 12

cortar (v) **26** 11, **31** 6, **31** 9

cortar el césped **26** 6

cortar la grama **26** 6

corte **43** B

cortina **32** 10, **99** 1

cortina de baño **34** 5

cortinas **28** 23

cortinero **34** 1

cortinilla **33** 1

costillas **10** 10

costura **101** A, **101** 10

costurera **84** 6

cotonete **33** 10

cotorro **64** 16

crema de afeitar **23** 22

cremera **29** 24

crimen y castigo **43**

crin de caballo **67** 21a

crisantemo **60** 4

cruce **44** 11

cruce de trébol **53** 4

cuaderno de espiral **76** 15

cuadrado **79** 9

cuadrilátero **94** 17

cuadro **28** 4

cuadro médico **39** 10

el cuarto de servicios **35**

el cuarto del bebé **33**

cuarto menguante **74** 25

cubeta **35** 15, **90** 16

cubeta de hielo **30** 21

cubículo **83** 5

cubierta **58** 22

cubierta de vuelo **75** 10

cubito **90** 16

cubo **35** 15, **79** 27

cucaracha **63** 9

cuchara **29** 8

cuchara (de albañil) **27** 27

cuchillo **29** 15

cucubano **63** 17

cuello **4** 4, **20** 20

cuenta **16** 14

cuerda **46** 20, **58** 25, **89** 23, **98** 10a

cuerdo de remolque **59** 11

cuerno **66** 16a, **67** 35a

el cuerpo **4** A

el cuerpo humano **4**, **5**

cuervo **64** 3

cuesto abajo de esquiar **95** C

cuidado médico y dental **39**

culebra **65** 9

cumbre **79** 21

cuna **33** 4

cuna mecedora **33** 26

cuñada **3** 8

cuñado **3** 11

cuneta **45** 26

cuota **55** 21

curita **39** 4

curva **79** 3

Dakota del norte **73** 34

Dakota del sur **73** 41

dar **17** 9

dátil **9** 22

de (la cancha de golf) **103** 10

dedo de enmedio **4** 26

debajo de (el escritorio) **102** 8

decoración **99** 2

de bolitas **24** 19

de cuadritos **24** 18

dedal **101** 21

dedo del pie **5** 54

dedo gordo del pie **5** 53

(dedo) pulgar **4** 24

defensa **52** 10

defensa delantera **51** 51

defensa derecha **93** 28

defensa izquierda **93** 26

defensa trasera **51** 42

delantal **16** 6

Delaware **72** 8

delfín **68** 13

delineador **23** 33

de lineas (rayitas) **24** 17

demandado **43** 23

dentista **39** 17

dentro de (el cajón) **102** 7

deportes en equipo **92**

deportes individuales **94**

depósito **15** 16

depresor de lengua **40** 12a

depunto **101** 26

desagüe **27** 10, **34** 9

desagüe de lluvia **27** 18

desarmador **37** 24

desarmador Phillips **37** 25

descansa brazo **50** 3

descanso en cama **41** 1

descripción de ropa **24**

descripción del clima **25**

desde (la cancha de golf) **103** 10

desembarcadero **58** 28

desengrapador **83** 29

desiertos **71**

deslizador de vela **59** 14

deslizador **57** 6

deslizarse **97** 12

despegue **57** B

despertador **32** 8

destapa caños **35** 14

destapador **30** 6

destello **100** 7

destornillador **37** 24

detective **43** 2

detector de humo **33** 15

detector de metales **56** 10

detergente **35** 25

detrás de (la silla) **102** 9

diagonal **79** 20

diamante de béisbol **93** A

diámetro **79** 12

dibujar **77** 11

diccionario **47** 24

diente **4** 42

diente de ajo **7** 25a

dinero **13**

dique **58** 28

dirección **46** 11

dirigible **57** 5

disc jockey **86** 9

disco compacto **100** 27

disco de (hule duro) hockey **92** 17

discos **100** 23

diseñador de moda **86** 6

diseño a cuadros **24** 22

disparar **97** 16

Distrito de Columbia **73** 51

división central **53** 18

divisor **53** 18

dobladillo **101** 11

doblar **38** 1

doctor **39** 11

documentación recibida **83** 12

dolor de cabeza **40** 6

dolor de espalda **40** 8

dolor de estómago **40** 7

dolor de garganta **40** 12

dolor de muela **40** 9

drenaje **34** 9

ducha **34** 4

dunas de arena **90** 12

durazno **9** 37

echar **31** 4

echar clavados **97** 14

eclipse lunar **74** 6

eclipse solar **74** 10

ecuador **71** 70

edificio de oficinas **44** 1

eje **50** 13

Ejército **48** 15

ejote(s) **6** 15

electricidad **80** 32

el, la electricista **85** 6

electrónica y fotografía **100**

elefante **66** 17

elevador **80** 9, **45** 17

elote **6** 12a

embrague **50** 25

embudo **78** 17

empeine **5** 51

empleado de biblioteca **47** 1

empleado de limpieza **49** 7, **85** 9

empleado postal **46** 14

empleados de negocios **86** C

empujar **26** 12

en (la ventana) **102** 1

en la playa **90**, **91**

enagua **22** 8

enarenar **26** 14

encendedor **16** 30

encender **17** 13

encendido **50** 14

enchufe **32** 26b, **36** 6

enciclopedia **47** 25

energía **80**,**80** A, **80** 24

enfermedades y heridas **40**

enfermera **39** 19

enfermero **42** 7

engrane **52** 20

engrapadora **83** 27

enredadera **61** 42

ensalada **18** 13

ensaladera **29** 25

entablado **90** 1

entero **79** 29

entero (color) **24** 20

entrada de carro **27** 1

entrar **77** 14

entre (los cojines) **102** 4

entrega de correo **46** A

entrenador **93** 21

entresuelo **99** 13

envase **12** 2

envases, cantidades, y dinero **12**, **13**

enyesado **39** 5

equipaje **56** 8

equipo (de alpinismo) **89** 27

escabroso **95** 6

escala **14** 7, **78** 4

escálamo **59** 21

escalera **28** 12, **35** 1, **42** 1

escalofrios **40** 4

escalón **28** 13

escalope **11** 35, **62** 10

escape **52** 33

escape de incendio **42** 4

escarabajo **63** 10

escenario **99** 5

esfera **47** 19

escoba **35** 7

escribir **77** 7

escribir a máquina **77** 10

escritor **86** 7

escritorio **28** 14, **76** 16, **83** 13

escuchar **77** 6

escudo **43** 5

escupidera **33** 33

escupidero **39** 16

escurridor **30** 2

esmalte para uñas **23** 25

esófago **5** 61

espacio exterior **74** A

espagueti **18** 10

espalda **4** 11

espantapájaros **81** 19

espárragos **6** 18

espátula **27** 21, **36** 14

espejo **32** 5

espejo lateral **50** 2

espejo retrovisor **50** 7

espina **60** 18c

espina dorsal **5** 58

espinaca **6** 8

esponja **34** 7

esposa **2** 4

esposas **43** 4

esposo **2** 3, **3** 12

esquí **95** 17

esquiador **59** 10, **94** 35

esquiando a campo traviesa **94**

esquina **44** 3

esquíes **94** 33

estaca **89** 30

estación **55** 18

estación de carga **58** 29

estación de policía **43** A

estación del metro **44** 16

estación del subterráneo **44** 16

estación espacial **75** 1

estacionamiento **45** 19

Los Estados Unidos **72**, **73**

estambre **101** 31

estampado **24** 21

estampilla **46** 10

estanque (de patos) **87** 8

estante **14** 6, **47** 17, **78** 8

estante de bicicleta **52** 14

este **71** 73

estéreo **28** 20

estetoscopio **39** 9

el, la estilista **84** 10

estómago **5** 66

estrella **74** 4

estuche de disección **78** 33

el, la estudiante **76** 19

estufa **30** 30

estufa de campamento **89** 25

etiqueta **46** 21

eucalipto **61** 27

Europa **70** 3

excavar **26** 3

excursionistas **88** 2

excusado **34** 29

explorador espacial **75** 4

extensible **23** 11

extensión **36** 5

extinguidor **42** 11

fagot **98** 14

faisán **64** 19

faja **22** 15

falcón **64** 7

falda **21** 36

familia de Mary Smith **3**

la familia **3**

farmacéutica **84** 1

farmacia **45** 22

faro **58** 14

fases de la luna **74** C

ficha de reclamo **47** 12

fiebre **40** 2

figuras geométricas **79** B

figuras sólidas **79** C

fila **47** 11, **81** 18

filete **11** 28

filtro **51** 52

fiscal acusador **43** 17

flama **29** 26, **78** 21

flamingo **64** 29

flanqueador **93** 31

flash **100** 7

flauta **98** 13

flojo **24** 4

flor de nochebuena **60** 15

flores **60**

Florida **72** 9

el florista **84** 11

flotador inflable **59** 20

foca **68** 12

foco **35** 22

fogata **89** 31

fondo entero **22** 10

foro **99** 5

fósforos **16** 28

fotocopiadora **47** 18, **83** 24

fotografía **100** B

fotógrafo **86** 4

fotos **100** 11

fracciones **79** D

fractura **40** 15

frambuesas **8** 16

frasco **12** 9, **78** 2

freir **31** 15

freno **50** 26, **52** 17

freno de emergencia **50** 15

freno manual **52** 24

frente **4** 32, **23** 18

frente a (la chimenea) **102** 6

fresa **8** 15

fresco **25** 9

frijoles cocidos **18** 3

frijol(es) negro(s) **6** 14

frío **25** 10

frisbee **90** 13

frontón con raqueta **94**

frontón de mano **94**

frutas **8, 9**

frutas cítricas **8**

frutas pequeñas **8**

frutas secas **9**

frutas y legumbres **14** 9

fuego **28** 9, **42** 5

fuente **87** 19

fuentes de fuerza **80** A

fuera de (el agua) **103** 7

Fuerza Aérea **48** 19

funda **15** 25, **32** 15, **43** 8

fuselaje **57** 14

fútbol **92**, **92** 13

gabinete **30** 22

gafas **21** 44

gafas de sol **90** 14

gajo **8** 8a

galaxia **74** 1

galleta **18** 22

gallo **64** 21

ganado **81** 12

gancho **23** 18, **32** 1, **36** 16

gancho para ropa **32** 2

Ganges **71** 67

ganso **64** 26

garaje **27** 2

gardenia **60** 14

garganta **5** 59

garra **68** 2a, **69** 29a

gas natural **80** 29

gas propano **80** 30

gasolina **80** 28

gatillo **48** 22

gatito **68** 5

gato **51** 38, **68** 4

gaveta **47** 5

gaveta para guante **50** 20

gavetero **32** 30

gavetes **20** 7

gaviota **64** 4

gaza **39** 25

gemelos **90** 7

generador eléctrico **80** 21

género **101** 4

gente y parentesco **2**

Georgia **72** 10

gerente **83** 18

geyser **80** 5

gimnasia **94**

el, la gimnasta **94** 23

girafa **67** 29

girasol **60** 19

giro de postal **46** 18

gis **76** 10

globo **47** 19, **57** 1

Gobi **71** 54

gol **92** 25

golf **94**

golfista **94** 10

Golfo de Alaska **70** 17

Golfo de Guinea **70** 25

Golfo de México **70** 19

Golfo Pérsico **70** 28

golpe **40** 17

golpear **96** 1

goma **50** 37, **52** 28, **76** 21, **78** 18

gorila **69** 17

gorrión **64** 10

gorra **19** 2, **21** 43, **92** 11

gorro de baño **34** 3

gorro de esquiar **19** 16

gotas para los ojos **41** 10

gotera **27** 10

gotero **78** 26

grabadora **100** 22

gráfico **78** 11

grama **27** 15

granada (de mano) **48** 29

grande **24** 8

granero **81** 5

granja de trigo **81** B

granja lechera **81** A

la granja y el rancho **81**

granjero **81** 7

(granos de) avena **60** 23

grapadora **83** 27

gratinar **31** 2

grillo **63** 5

grosellas **8** 11

grúa **49** 2, **58** 6

grupo (musical) de Rock **99** C

guagua **54** A

guante **27** 20, **92** 12, **94** 11, **94** 15

guante del cácher **92** 4

guante entero **19** 11

guantera **50** 20

guantes **19** 1

guantes de trabajo **27** 26

el, la guarda **88** 5

el, la guarda parques **88** 5

el guardia de seguridad **56** 9

guardia de seguridad **86** 14

guarniciones **89** 22

guía **50** 8
guiar **97** 15
guineo **9** 20
guitarra **98** 11
guitarra eléctrica **99** 26
guitarrista principal **99** 25
gusano de seda **63** 1
haba(s) **6** 16
habichuela(s) **6** 13
habichuelas cocidas **18** 3
habichuela(s) tiernas **6** 15
hacer (la cama) **38** 8
hacha **36** 17, **42** 14
hacia (la cancha de golf) **103** 9
hacia (el hoyo) **103** 4
hacia abajo de (la colina) **103** 3
hacia arriba de (la colina) **103** 11
hacia dentro de (el hoyo) **103** 12
halcón **64** 7
hamaca **27** 11
hamburguesa **18** 9
el hangar **57** 17
harmónica **98** 30
harpa **98** 6
Hawaii **72** 11
hebilla **20** 17
helado **18** 36, **25** 11, **25** 16
helando **25** 11
hélice **57** 2a
helicóptero **57** 2
hermana **3** 10
hermano **3** 9
hervir **31** 16
hiedra venenosa **61** 45
hielera **91** 41
hiena **69** 30
hierba(s) **69**
hígado **5** 65
higienista bucal **39** 14
higo **9** 21
hija **3** 15
hijo **3** 16
(carrete de) hilo **101** 2
Himalayas **71** 47
hipopótamo **66** 14
hipotenusa **79** 24
hockey sobre hielo **92**

hogaza de pan **12** 7
hoja de música **98** 2
hoja **61** 36a, **94** 27
(hojas sueltas de) papel **76** 13
holgado **24** 4
hombre **2** 2
hombro **4** 5
hongo(s) **7** 30
horario **55** 20
hormiga **63** 12
hornear **31** 14
hornilla **30** 29
horno microondas **30** 23
horno **30** 32
horquilla **59** 21
hot dog **18** 2
hoyo **94** 8
Huang **71** 68
huellas digitales **43** 24
huerta **81** 1
hueso **9** 37a
huevo **64** 13
huevo estrellado **18** 32
humo **42** 15
Idaho **72** 12
iguana **65** 13
Illinois **72** 13
imán **78** 27
imperdibles **33** 11
impermeable **21** 38
impresiones **100** 11
impresora **83** 4
incendio **42** 5
Indiana **72** 14
índice **4** 25
Indico **70** 13
infección **40** 14
información **47** 22
ingeniero **55** 15
ingeniero de vuelo **56** 17
inodoro **34** 29
insectos **63**
insignia **43** 5
instrumentos **39** 13, **56** 14
instrumentos de cuerdas **98**
instrumentos de metal **98**
instrumentos de percusión **98**

instrumentos de viento **98**
instrumentos musicales **98**
interruptor **37** 43c
interruptor de luz **32** 25
intestinos **5** 67
invierno **26**
inyección **41** 8
Iowa **72** 15
iris **5** 47
jabón **34** 15
jabón de fregar **30** 10
jabón líquido para trastes **30** 10
jabonera **34** 6
jacinto **60** 10
jaiba(s) **11** 36
jalea **18** 31
jamón **10** 12
jardinero **85** 3
jarra **29** 4
jarrón **28** 6
jeep **48** 9
jeringa **39** 27
el jet **57** 18
jet privado **57** 3
(ji) tomate(s) **7** 19
jinete (profesional) **94** 21
jockey **94** 21
joroba **67** 33a
joyera **84** 12
joyería **23** A
joyería y cosméticos **23**
joyero **32** 4
juego de cubiertos **29** 22
juegos infantiles **87** 17
juey (es) **11** 36, **62** 9
juez **43** 10
juguetero **33** 29
junto a (la TV) **102** 11
Júpiter **74** 15
jurado **43** 21
Kansas **72** 16
Kentucky **72** 17
labio **4** 43
labor de gancho **101** 28
laboratorio de ciencias **78**
lacrosse **92**
lado **79** 10

lagartija **65** 15

lámpara **28** 28, **89** 29

lámpara (de mano) **35** 3

lana **101** 23

lancha **59** 18

lancha de motor **59** 13

lanchón **58** 12

langosta **11** 30, **62** 13

lanza agua **42** 17

lanzador **93** 12

lanzar **97** 10

lápiz **76** 24

lápiz labial **23** 29

lápiz para cejas **23** 26

larga **24** 2

largo **79** 36

las Fuerzas armadas **48**

lata rociadora **13** 24

lata **12** 10

latería **30** 15

lavabo **34** 19

lavadora **35** 30

lavandería **35** 28

lavamanos **34** 19

lavaplatos **30** 1

lavar **38** 16

levantar (la mano) **77** 1

lazo **58** 25

leche **14** 5

lechuga **6** 6, **6** 7

lechuza **64** 6

leer **77** 4

legumbres **6**, **7**

lejos de (el hoyo) **103** 5

Lena **71** 66

lengua **4** 41

lente **100** 6

lentes **21** 44

lentes de protección **94** 28

lentes de seguridad **78** 12

lentes para el sol **90** 14

leña **28** 10

león **68** 3

leopardo **68** 1

letrero **44** 8

letrero de carretera **53** 23

letrero de límite de velocidad **53** 8

letrero de salida **53** 24

libélula **63** 4

libra de pan **12** 7

librería **45** 18

librero **28** 22, **83** 20

librito **13** 17

libro (de texto) **76** 26

licuadora **30** 12

liguero **22** 14

lija **37** 27

lima **8** 10, **23** 24

limón **8** 9

limpia calles **49** 1

limpia parabrisas **50** 6

limpiador **50** 6

limpiador de esponja **35** 6

limpiador en polvo **35** 9

limpiamesas **16** 3

limpiar **17** 6, **26** 2, **38** 5

limpio **24** 6

línea de fuera **93** 9, **95** 4

línea del saque **95** 3

línea recta **79** 1

lineas **79** A

líneas de corriente **80** 24

líneas paralelas **79** 4

líneas perpendiculares **79** 2

linterna **89** 29

líquido limpia ventanas **35** 10

lirio **60** 11

listado **83** 8

llama **29** 26, **66** 15

llanta **50** 37, **52** 28

llanta de repuesto **51** 39

llanta inflable **91** 29

llave de perro **36** 10

llave de tuercas **36** 10

llave del agua caliente **34** 17

llave del agua fría **34** 18

llave inglesa **36** 12

llenar **26** 9

lluvioso **25** 1

lobo **69** 29

loción para bebé **33** 6

loción para después de afeitar **23** 21

loción para el sol **91** 39

locker **76** 6

locutor de noticiero **86** 2

lombriz **62** 11

lonchera **21** 31

longaniza **10** 7

loro **64** 16

loseta **34** 27

Louisiana **72** 18

loza **29** 1

luces delanteras **51** 48

luces direccionales **51** 50

luces para estacionarse **51** 49

luciérnaga **63** 17

luna **74** 9

luna llena **74** 24

luna nueva **74** 26

luneta **99** 12

lupa **78** 15

lustrar **38** 3

luz de reversa **50** 30

luz del freno **50** 29

luz trasera **50** 31

macana **43** 9

madeja **101** 24

madera **36** 4

madras **24** 22

madre **3** 4

maestra **76** 4

magnolia **61** 29

mahón **19** 6

Maine **72** 19

maíz **60** 24

malecón **58** 3

maleta **56** 7

maletera **51** 40

maletero **56** 5

maletín **21** 37

mamadera **33** 18

mameluco **21** 30

mamíferos I **66**, **67**

mamíferos II **68**, **69**

mamíferos acuáticos **68**

mamíferos de bolsa, sin dientes, y voladores **66**

mamíferos de pezuña **66**

(manada de) ganado **81** 20

mancuernas **23** 12

mandadero **86** 19

mandíbula **4** 38

mandolina **98** 4

mandril **69** 19

manejar **97** 15

manga corta **20** 21

manga larga **20** 15

mango **8** 5

manguera **27** 14, **42** 8, **51** 57

maní **9** 28

manija **50** 4

la mano **4** B

mantaraya **65** 6

mantel **29** 16

mantequilla **18** 18

mantis **63** 7

manubrios (de carreras) **52** 2

manubrios de viaje **52** 12

manzana **8** 2

mapa del mundo **70**, **71**

mapache **68** 7

máquina de coser **101** 1

máquina de escribir **83** 10

máquina de lavar platos **30** 1

Mar Amarillo **70** 37

Mar Arábigo **70** 30

Mar Báltico **70** 22

Mar Caribe **70** 20

Mar Caspiano **70** 27

Mar de Barents **70** 23

Mar de Beaufort **70** 15

Mar de Bering **70** 34

Mar de Kara **70** 31

Mar de Laptev **70** 33

Mar de Okhotsk **70** 35

Mar del Caribe **70** 20

Mar del Este de China **70** 38

Mar del Japón **70** 36

Mar del Norte **70** 21

Mar del Sur de China **70** 39

Mar Mediterráneo **70** 24

Mar Negro **70** 26

Mar Rojo **70** 29

marañón(es) **9** 27

maraquita **33** 21

maravilla **60** 6

marcador **55** 23

marco **28** 4

mares, golfos y bahías **70**

margarita **60** 5

Marina **48** 13, **48** 17

marinero **48** 14

marino **48** 18

mariposa **63** 3

mariposa nocturna **63** 21

mariquita **63** 14

mariscal de campo **93** 32

mariscos **11** D

marquesina **27** 2

Marte **74** 14

martillo **36** 13, **43** 12

Maryland **72** 20

máscara **23** 28

máscara del cácher **92** 3

Massachusetts **72** 21

mástil **59** 8

materia **47** 10

material **101** 4

matemáticas **79**

mazo **36** 11

(mazo de) paja **81** 13

mazorca de maíz **6** 12

mecánico **84** 2

mecanógrafa **83** 6

medias **22** 6, **22** 7

medias de invierno **19** 14

medicina **41**

medidas **79** E

medidor **55** 23

medidor de (la) gasolina **50** 9

medidor de tiempo **78** 13

medio **4** 26

medio fondo **22** 8

medio pollo **11** 17

medio trasero **93** 33

medios de comunicación y las artes **86** A

medusa **62** 12

mejilla **4** 35

mejillón(es) **11** 34

melocotón **9** 37

melón **9** 26, **9** 36

melón (verde) **9** 35

menear **31** 1

mensajero **85** 10, **86** 19

mentón **4** 3

menú **16** 7

meñique **4** 28

meple **61** 38

mercado de frutas y legumbres **45** 28

Mercurio **74** 11

mesa **29** 7

mesa de día de campo **88** 15

mesa de planchar **35** 13

mesa de reconocimiento **39** 6

mesa de trabajo **36** 22, **78** 24

mesera **16** 2

mesera (de bebidas) **16** 32

mesero **16** 5

meseta **88** 1

mesita **28** 29, **56** 22

mesita central **28** 26

mesita de noche **32** 27

mesita (portátil) **33** 9

meta **95** 21

meteoro **74** 5

metro **54** B

mezanine **99** 13

mezcladora de cemento **49** 13

Michigan **72** 22

mico **69** 14

microfilm **47** 13

microscopio **78** 30

mina de carbón **80** 6

mini-cámara **100** 2

mini-computadora **100** 31

Minnesota **72** 23

Misisipí **71** 58, **72** 24

Missouri **73** 25

mitón **19** 11

mocasín **21** 42

mochila **19** 4

mochila con armazón **89** 28

el, la modela **86** 5, **101** 7

módulo de comando **75** 9

módulo lunar **75** 7

mojado **25** 15

mojarra **65** 7

Mojave **71** 48

molde **30** 24

moler **31** 2

molinete **58** 23

molino de viento **80** 19

moluscos **11**

molusco(s) bivalvo(s) **11** 35

mondar **31** 5

moneda de cinco **13** 28

moneda de diez **13** 29

moneda de veinticinco **13** 30

monedas **13** 26

monitor **100** 32

mono de Asia **69** 15

monoriel **55** 29

Montana **73** 26

montaña **89** 19

Montañas Apalaches **71** 41

Montañas Cáucaso **71** 45

Montañas Rocallosas **71** 40

Montes Apalaches **71** 41

Montes Urales **71** 46

montículo **93** 11

moras **8** 12

morsa **68** 11

mortero **48** 28

mosca **63** 18

mosquitero **27** 19

mosquito **63** 13

mostaza **18** 1

mostrador **29** 29, **30** 27

mostrador de chequeo **15** 26, **47** 2

mostrador de fiambre y quesos **14** 1

motel **90** 3

moto pequeña **52** 29

motocicleta **52** 30, **53** 19

motor **51** F, **52** 32

motor exterior **59** 12

móvil **33** 2

mozo **56** 5

muchacha **2** 9

muchacho **2** 8

muchacho de los bates **93** 18

mudador **49** 12

mueble de pared **28** 19

muelle **58** 3

muestra en transparencia **78** 31

mujer **2** 1

muleta **39** 7

muñeca **4** 21, **33** 28

murciélago **66** 4

músculo **5** 62

música, baile/danza y teatro **99**

músico **99** 10

muslo **4** 18, **11** 19

nabo **7** 34

nadador **91** 28

nalgas **4** 15

naranja **8** 8

narciso **60** 8

nariz **4** 36, **57** 8

navajas para afeitar **23** 23

Naval **48** 13

naves espaciales **75** A

(con) neblina **25** 12

Nebraska **73** 27

nectarín **8** 17

Neptuno **74** 18

Nevada **73** 28

(con) nevado **25** 3

nevaja **94** 27

nevera **30** 19, **91** 41

nido **64** 31

nieta **2** 11

nieto **2** 12

(con) nieve **25** 3

Níger **71** 61

Nilo **71** 63

niña **2** 9

niño **2** 8

niños **2** 7

nochero **32** 27

norte **71** 71

Norteamérica **70** 1

nublado **25** 2

núcleo **80** 14

nudillo **4** 22

nueces **9**

nueva **24** 13

Nueva Hampshire **73** 29

Nueva Jersey **73** 30

Nueva York **73** 32

Nuevo México **73** 31

nuez (nueces) de nogal **9** 29

número de clasificación **47** 7

número del edificio **45** 24

nutria **68** 10

ñame **7** 24

Ob **71** 64

oboe **98** 15

obscuro **24** 10

océanos **70**

el, la oculista **84** 9

ocupaciones I: La calle principal en los Estados Unidos **84**

ocupaciones II **85**

ocupaciones III **86**

oeste **71** 74

oficial **86** 13

oficial de la corte **43** 19

(oficial de) policía **43** 6

oficina **83**

oficina de correo **44** 9

oficina de correos **46** B

Ohio **73** 35

oído **4** 34

ojal **101** 8

el ojo **5** D

ojo morado **40** 5

Oklahoma **73** 36

ola **91** 24

olla **30** 8, **30** 13

olmo **61** 36

operadora de conmutador **83** 1

operario **85** 12

el, la optico **84** 9

orangután **69** 18

órbita **74** 21

orden monetaria **46** 18

ordenar **17** 5

Oregon **73** 37

oreja **4** 34

orejeras **19** 10

órgano **98** 29

los órganos internos **5** F

orificio nasal **4** 37

orilla de la carretera **53** 22

orillero **33** 5

orquesta **99** 6

orquídea **60** 12

orza de deriva **59** 6

oso de peluche **33** 3

oso hormiguero **66** 5

(oso) Koala **66** 1

oso negro **69** 21

oso panda **69** 20

oso pardo **69** 23
oso polar **69** 22
osos **69**
ostión(es) **11** 33
ostra(s) **11** 33, **62** 2
Otoño **26**
otras actividades de costura **101** B
otras formas de transporte **55** E
otras plantas **61**
otros instrumentos **98**
óvalo **79** 18
oveja **10** 13, **67** 25
oveja pequeña **67** 24
ovejas **81** 10
overol **21** 30
paciente **39** 20
Pacífico del norte **70** 9
Pacífico del sur **70** 10
padre **3** 5
padres **2** 6
pagar **17** 7
paja **81** 13
pájaro azul **64** 8
pájaro carpintero **64** 17
pájaros **64**
pala **27** 31, **90** 17
pala de jardín **27** 27
pala de nieve **49** 5
palanca de cambios **50** 17
palanca de direccionales **50** 11
palanca de velocidades **50** 24, **52** 22
palco **99** 11
palear **26** 13
paleta **40** 12a, **94** 18
paleta (de agua) **59** 3
palitos **98** 19a
palitos de algodón **33** 10
palma **4** 29
palmera **61** 26
palo **94** 9
palo de cortina **34** 1
palo de hockey **92** 18
palo largo **94** 34, **95** 14
paloma **64** 1
palos de golf **95** 5
palta **9** 33
pan **14** 12

pan tostado **18** 34
panadería **44** 6
panadero **84** 8
pancakes **18** 5
páncreas **5** 71
pandereta **98** 17
panecillo **18** 7, **18** 19, **18** 27
panqueques **18** 5
pantaleta **22** 12
pantaleta (bikini) **22** 11
pantalla **100** 14
pantalla de gancho **23** 16
pantalla de lámpara **28** 27
pantalla de pinchar **23** 15
pantallas **23** 1
pantalón **20** 4
pantalón de mezclilla **19** 6
pantalón (de pana) **21** 27
pantalón de sudadera **20** 10
pantaloncillo **20** 14
pantalones impermeables para
    pescar **88** 10
pantimedia **22** 5
pantorrilla **4** 20
pants **20** 10
pantuflas **22** 18
pañal **33** 13
pañal desechable **33** 12
paño de platos **30** 18
pañuelos faciales **32** 13
papa al horno **18** 20
papalote **91** 22
papas fritas **18** 4, **18** 28
papas majadas **18** 17
papaya **8** 6
papa(s) **7** 23
papel absorbente **35** 23
papel de baño **34** 30
papel de gráficas **78** 11
papel filtro **78** 16
papel higiénico **34** 30
papitas **18** 4
paquete **12** 4, **13** 16, **46** 19
(paquete) correo express **46** 23
paquete de seis **13** 13
(paquetito de) azúcar **16** 13
paramédico **42** 7

el parabrisas **51** 45
paracaídas **48** 6
parada de autobús **44** 13
paraguas **20** 24
Paraná **71** 60
parasol **90** 21
pared **28** 3
párpado **5** 45
parque **87** 15
parques del vecindario **87**
parquímetro **45** 20
parrilla **27** 22, **88** 12
parte superior del brazo **4** 7
partidura **4** 31
pasa(s) **9** 24
pasaje **56** 4
pasajero **54** 6, **55** 25
pasamano **28** 11
pasar **96** 5
pascua **60** 15
pase de abordar **56** 18
paseo por agua **59**
pasillo **14** 10, **56** 23, **76** 12
paso a desnivel **53** 3
pasta de dientes **34** 16
pastelería **44** 6
pastelillo de fresa **18** 26
pastilla **13** 18
pastisal **81** 6
pasto **27** 15
pastor **69** 28
pastura **81** 6
pata **10** 14, **11** 20, **69** 29a
pata de foca **68** 12a
patas frontales **66** 3d
patas traseras **66** 3b
patear **96** 3
patilla **4** 33
patín **94** 26
patinaje en hielo **94**
patinar **97** 9
patines de hielo **19** 15
patio **27** 17
el patio interior **27** C
pato **11** 25, **64** 25
patrón **101** 7
pavo **11** 23, **64** 20

pavo real **64** 18

peaje **53** 27

peatón **44** 12

peces **65** A

peces y reptiles **65**

pecho **4** 12

pechicolorado **64** 9

pechuga **11** 21

pedal **39** 18, **52** 19

pedazo **13** 22

pega **76** 17

pegamento **37** 33, **76** 17

pegar **96** 1

peine **32** 6

peinilla **32** 6

pelar **31** 5

pelícano **64** 24

película **100** C

pelo **4** 30

pelota de playa **90** 11

pelota de softball **92** 10

peluquero **84** 3

Pennsylvania **73** 38

pensamiento **60** 2

pepinillo **18** 8

pepino(s) **7** 20

pepita **8** 8c

pequeña Liga de béisbol **92**

pequeño **24** 7

pequeño dedo del pie **5** 55

pequeño jugador de liga **92** 8

pera **8** 18

perfume **23** 27

perico **64** 16

periódico **21** 48

periquito **64** 15

periscopio **48** 8

perno **37** 38

perro caliente **18** 2

perro cobrador **69** 26

perro de aguas **69** 24

perros **69**

persianas **32** 12

persona de entrega **49** 10

persona que viaja pidiendo aventón **53** 9

personal **48** B

pesa **14** 17, **34** 32

pesa balanza **78** 4

pesas **78** 5

pesca **88**

pescado **11** 26

pescado entero **11** 27

pescador **58** 2

peseta **13** 30

pestañas **5** 46

pétalo **60** 18b

petirrojo **64** 9

petit pois **6** 17

petunia **60** 7

pez espada **65** 3

pez estrella **62** 7

pezón **33** 18

pezuña **67** 35b

piano **98** 1

picada **40** 3

picador **30** 26

picar **31** 11

pichón **64** 1

pico **64** 3a, **64** 24a, **89** 20

picolo **98** 12

el pie **5** E

pie de la cama **32** 24

pierna **10** 14, **11** 20, **4** 17

pieza **13** 22

pieza del patrón **101** 6

pijamas **22** 19

píldora **41** 7

piloto **56** 15

pimentero **29** 9

pimiento(s) **7** 22

pinches de ropa **35** 20

pincitas **78** 32

ping-pong **94**

pingüino **64** 27

pino **61** 34, **94** 5

Pintado **71** 49

pintar **26** 1

pintora **85** 7

pintura **28** 5, **37** 31

pinza **62** 13a

pinzas **35** 20, **36** 19, **78** 28, **78** 29

piña **8** 4

pipa **16** 26

piquete de insecto **40** 3

pirámide **79** 25

piso **32** 29

pista **57** 19, **94** 25, **94** 32

pista de carreras **95** D

pista para correr **87** 9

pistola **43** 7

pitillo **16** 10

pizarra **76** 5

pizarrón **76** 5

pizza **18** 30

placa **50** 28

plancha **35** 12

planchar **38** 11

planeador **57** 4

planeador de mar **91** 25

planeador pequeño de agua **91** 27

los planetas **74**

plantar **26** 4

plantas caseras **61** 39

plantas venenosas **61**

plantas y árboles **60**, **61**

plataforma **54** 11

plataforma de despegue **75** 15

plátanos **9** 20

platillo **29** 21, **90** 13

platillos **98** 18

platito **29** 21

platito de muestras **78** 3

platito para mantequilla y pan **29** 11

plato **29** 13

plato hondo **13** 23

plomera **85** 1

pluma **64** 7.a

pluma atómica **76** 22

plumero **35** 2

Plutón **74** 19

podar **26** 8

podio **99** 7

policía de tránsito **44** 10

pollería **11** B

pollito **64** 22

pollo **11** 24, **64** 23

pollo entero **11** 16

pollo frito **18** 29

pompa **13** 14, **52** 21

pompa de aire **53** 13

pompa de gasolina **53** 14

pompón **60** 13

poner la mesa **17** 8

ponero **53** 9

pony **67** 20

popa **58** 11

popote **16** 10, **78** 14

por encima de (el gato negro) **102** 2

porche **27** 6

porristas **93** 20

porta autos **49** 17

porta bustos **22** 13

porta carga **58** 4

porta compras **15** 19

porta ropa **56** 1

porta vaso **16** 27

portafolio **21** 37

portalón **58** 20

portaviones **48** 4

portero **85** 11, **92** 24

portilla **58** 21

poste de luz **45** 29

poste de servicio **80** 26

poste del gol **93** 35

pote **12** 9

potro **67** 22

pozo petrolero **80** 1

(pozo) tiro de elevador **80** 10

prendas **23** A

prendedor **23** 13, **23** 8

prender **17** 13

preposiciones de descripción **102**

preposiciones de movimiento **103**

presa **80** 18

presillas **101** 14

presión alta **40** 10

primates **69**

primavera **26**

primer cuarto **74** 23

primera base **93** 8

primo **3** 7

prisma **78** 1

proa **58** 5

procesador de palabras **83** 7

producción de energía **80** B

productos enlatados **14** 13

productos lácteos **14** 4

profundidad **79** 33

el programa espacial **75**

programador (de computadora) **86** 16

programas **99** 17

pronosticador del tiempo **86** 1

propina **55** 22

proveta **78** 9

proyector **100** 16

proyector de transparencias **100** 13

púa **66** 11a

publicaciones periódicas **47** 15

puerco espín **66** 11

el puerto **58**

puerta de carga **57** 13

puerta de salida **95** 20

puesto de periódicos y revistas **45** 30

puesto de refrescos **90** 2

pulidora **37** 26

pulir **38** 3

pulmón **5** 63

pulpo **62** 6

pulsera **23** 9

puntada **101** 19

puntadas **39** 21

punteado **24** 19

punto de partida **95** 13

puntos **39** 21

pupila **5** 48

puré de papas **18** 17

quemacoco **51** 44

quemador **30** 29, **78** 20

quemadura **40** 18

quemar **17** 14

quijada **4** 38

quilla **59** 6

rábano(s) **7** 29

radiador **51** 56

radio **50** 18, **79** 14

raíz **61** 35d

rama **61** 35a

ramita **61** 33a

rana **65** 17

rancho **81** C

ranura **46** 13

ranurador **37** 37

rápidos de río **89** 17

raqueta **94** 2, **94** 18, **94** 29

raqueta de lacrosse **92** 16

rasgar **77** 9

raspar **26** 15

rastrillar **26** 10

rastrillo **23** 20, **27** 30

rata **66** 7

ratón **66** 9

ratonera **35** 32

raya **4** 31

rayado **24** 17

rayo **52** 26

rayos x (equis) **39** 1

reactor nuclear **80** 13

rebanada **13** 21

rebanar **31** 10

reborde **45** 26

rebotar **97** 11

el, la recepcionista **86** 17

receptor **92** 2, **93** 16, **100** 21

recibidor **44** 2

recibo **15** 20, **55** 24

reclinador **28** 16

recogedor **35** 8

recoger **17** 6, **26** 7

recortar **26** 8

rectángulo **79** 19

red **92** 23, **95** 2

red de pesca **88** 9

red metálica **78** 6

refacción **51** 39

refinería **80** 12

reflector **52** 25, **99** 4

refajo **22** 10

refresco **16** 11

refrigerador **30** 19

regadera **27** 13, **34** 4

regadera de mano **27** 16

regar **26** 5

registro en el aeropuerto **56**

regla de carpintero **36** 1

regla **76** 23

reloj **76** 2

reloj de pulsera **23** 10

remitente **46** 8

remo **59** 3, **59** 22

remolacha **7** 33

remolcador **58** 13

renacuajo **65** 16

reparación y mantenimiento **85** A
reparar **38** 10
repisa **28** 7, **47** 26
repisa del gis **76** 9
repollo **6** 3
reportero **86** 11
repostería **14** 11
repuesta **51** 39
repuesto **35** 11
resbaladilla **87** 12
resfriado **40** 11
resfrío **40** 11
resfríos **40** 4
respaldo **50** 35
respirador **91** 34
restorán familiar **16** A
restorán familiar y bar **16**
restregar **38** 2
retroproyector **76** 27
revista **47** 16
revolvedora de cemento **49**
revolver **31** 1
revólver **43** 7
Rhode Island **73** 39
ribete **95** 16
riendas **94** 22
rifle **48** 21
rinoceronte **66** 16
riñón **5** 70
Río Grande **71** 57
ríos **71**
robalo **65** 7
roble **61** 33
roble venenoso **61** 43
rocas **88** 11
rociador **27** 13, **87** 14
rodilla **4** 19
rodillo **30** 25, **37** 29
roedores **66**
rollo **12** 11
rollo de película **100** 10
(rollo de) película **100** 17
rollo relleno de carne con verduras **18** 25
rolo **30** 25
rolodex **83** 14
rompecabezas **33** 31
romper **31** 7, **77** 9

rompeviento **19** 5
rondalla **37** 40
ropa de exteriores **19**
ropa del día **20**, **21**
ropa interior y de dormir **22**
ropero **32** 9
rosa **60** 18
rosbí **10** 8
rosbif **10** 8
rosca **37** 42b
Rubalcali **71** 52
rubor **23** 32
rueda **52** 4
ruedas de entrenamiento **52** 1
ruedo **101** 11
sábana **32** 19
sacacopias **47** 18
sacacorcho **16** 17
sacapuntas **76** 20, **83** 30
saco de vestir **21** 33
saco "sport" **20** 2
sacudidor **35** 2
sacudir **38** 15
Sahara **71** 51
la sala **28**
sala de juicio **43** B
salamandra **65** 14
salero **29** 10
salir **77** 13
salón de clase **76**
salsa de tomate **16** 4
saltamonte **63** 6
salvavidas (objeto) **90** 9
el, la salvavidas (persona) **90** 6
sanocochо **10** 4, **18** 14
sandalia **20** 19
sandía **9** 26
sandwich **16** 16
sarpullido **40** 1
sartén **30** 5
sastre **84** 6
satélite climatológico **75** 3
satélite de comunicación **75** 2
Saturno **74** 16
sauce **61** 31
saxofón **98** 24
secador **30** 18, **34** 26

secadora **35** 24
secar **38** 5, **38** 9
sección **79** 15
sección de carga **75** 9
sección de referencia **47** 21
sección de revistas **47** 15
sección del saque **95** 1
seco **25** 14
secoya **61** 25
secretaria **83** 11
sedán (dos puertas) **51** D
segadora trilladora **81** 17
segunda base **93** 7
seguridad **56**
seguro **33** 11, **50** 1, **52** 13
seleccionador de rayos **56** 11
sello de correo **46** 9
semáforo **45** 21
semilla **8** 8c, **9** 37a
señal luminosa preventiva **51** 41
sencillo **13** 29
serrote **36** 8
serrucho **36** 8, **36** 18
servicios domésticos **85** B
servilleta **29** 14
servir **17** 3, **31** 4, **96** 2
seta(s) **7** 30
shampú **34** 8
shorts **20** 14
shorts de baño **91** 33
sierra **36** 3
sierra circular **36** 20
sierra eléctrica **27** 25
Sierra Madre **71** 42
silbato **90** 5
silla **29** 17
silla de mecanógrafa **83** 17
silla de montar **94** 20
silla de playa **90** 20
silla de ruedas **39** 2
silla del salvavidas **90** 8
silla del testigo **43** 18
(silla) mecedora **33** 16
silla para niño **16** 8
sillita **16** 8
silo **81** 4
sinfonola **16** 12

sintetizador **99** 21

sintonizador **100** 21

sirga **59** 11

el sistema postal de los Estados
Unidos **46**

el sistema solar **74** B

sobaco **4** 10

sobre **83** 31, **102** 2

sobre (aéreo) **46** 16

sobre (la alfombra) **102** 5

sobre (la mesa) **102** 10

sobre (el puente) **103** 8

sobreabrigo **19** 20

sobrecama **32** 23

el, la sobrecargo **56** 20

sobrecito de azúcar **16** 13

sobretodo **19** 24

sobrina **3** 14

sobrino **3** 13

soga **89** 23

sofá **28** 25

softball **92**

sol **74** 7, **80** 3

solapa **20** 1

soldado **48** 16

soleadero **27** 24

soleado **25** 4

sólido **24** 20

sombra para ojos **23** 30

sombrero **19** 18

sombrero duro **21** 28

sombrilla **20** 24

sombrilla de playa **90** 21

sonaja **33** 21

soporte **39** 3, **52** 9

soporte del aro **78** 19

sorbeta **16** 10

sortija(s) **23** 2

sortija de boda **23** 4

sortija de compromiso **23** 3

sospechoso **43** 3

sostén **22** 13

sostén de ollas **30** 34

sostener **17** 12

spaniel **69** 24

suavizante **35** 27

subibaja **87** 18

submarino **48** 7

sucio **24** 5

sudadera **20** 8

Sudamérica **70** 2

suela **20** 6

suelto **24** 4

suéter abierto **21** 26

suéter cerrado **19** 7

suéter (cuello de tortuga) **19** 13

suéter (cuello V) **19** 23

sujeta papel **83** 28

sundae **18** 23

el supermercado **14**, **15**

sur **71** 72

surco **81** 18

suspensorio **22** 4

tabla **91** 25

tabla para cortar **30** 26

tablero **50** 19, **92** 19

tablero de anuncios **76** 7

tablero (de puntuación/puntaje) **93** 19

tablero para colgar herramientas **36** 15

tableta **41** 6

tablilla **47** 26, **50** 28

tablillo **14** 6

tablón de edictos **76** 7

tachuela **76** 25

taco **18** 24

tacón **20** 5

Takla Makan **71** 53

taladro **37** 43a, **39** 15

taladro de mano **36** 9

taladro eléctrico **37** 43

talco para bebé **33** 7

tallar **38** 2

taller de trabajo **36**, **37**

tallo **8** 2a, **60** 1a

talón **5** 50

tambor **98** 19

tambora **98** 21

tamborilero **99** 27

tamborina **98** 17

tanque **48** 10

tanque de gasolina **50** 34

tanque de oxígeno **91** 37

tapa **30** 9

tapabocina **50** 36

tapacubo **50** 36

tapete **32** 28, **50** 22

tapete de baño **34** 12

tapón **34** 10, **50** 36, **78** 10

taquilla **55** 19

taquilla de fichas **54** 13

tarifa **54** 5, **55** 21

tarjeta de biblioteca **47** 3

tarjeta informativa **47** 6

tarjeta postal **46** 17

tarjetero **47** 4

taxi **55** D, **55** 27

taxista **55** 26

taza **13** 19, **29** 20

tazón **13** 23, **78** 23

té **16** 15

teatro al aire libre **87** 2

techo **27** 4, **28** 2

teclado **98** 1a, **100** 33

técnica en reparación **84** 5

tee **95** 13

tejadillo de herramientas **27** 28

tejedora **101** 30

tejido **101** 22, **101** 30

tela **101** 4

telaraña **63** 15

teléfono **32** 26, **83** 15

teléfono público **44** 7

telescopio **74** 22

televisión **100** 5

televisor **28** 18, **100** 5

tema **47** 10

temperatura **25** 6

tenacillas **78** 32

tenazas **78** 28

tendedero **35** 19

tenedor **29** 12

tender (la cama) **38** 8

tenis **20** 11, **94**

Tennessee **73** 42

tentáculo **62** 12a

tercera base **93** 4

terminal **51** 55, **57** 16

termita **63** 11

termo **88** 14

termómetro **25** 5, **78** 22

ternero **67** 31

errier **69** 25

estigo **43** 13

etera **29** 19, **30** 28

etilla **33** 18

Texas **73** 43

ia **3** 6

iburón **65** 5

ienda de departamentos **44** 5

ierra **74** 8

Tierra **74** 13

igre **68** 2

ijeras de césped **27** 29

ijeras de piquitos **101** 5

imbal **98** 21

imbre (de correo) **46** 10

imón **59** 5

ina **34** 11

io **3** 3

ipos de correo **46** C

irar **97** 10

ítulo **47** 9

itabuzón **16** 17

iza **76** 10

oalla calentadora **41** 3

oalla de baño **34** 24

oalla de manos **34** 23

oalla de playa **90** 15

oallero **34** 25

oallita **34** 22

oallitas para bebé **33** 8

obillo **5** 49

oca cassettes **100** 25

oca discos compacto **100** 28

ocadiscos **100** 18

ocar **77** 2

ocineta **10** 11, **18** 33

ocino **10** 11, **18** 33

oldo **51** 47

omar **17** 10

opo **66** 8

orcedura **40** 13

ornamesa **100** 18

ornillo **37** 42

ornillo de banco **36** 2, **37** 36

ornillo grande **37** 38

orniquete de entrada **54** 12

orno **54** 12

toro **67** 34

toronja **8** 7

torre blindada de armas **48** 12

torre de control **57** 20

torre enfriadora **80** 16

torres transmisoras **80** 23

tortuga **65** 12

tortuga gigante **65** 18

tostada **18** 34

tostador **30** 16

trabajo en fábrica **85** C

trabajos manuales **101**

tractor **81** 15

trailer **49** 15

traje de baño **90** 18

traje de buceo **91** 38

traje de tres piezas **21** 40

traje espacial **75** 6

trajecito **33** 19

trampa de arena **95** 11

transacciones bancarias **86** B

transatlántico **58** 27

transbordador **58** 17

el transbordador espacial **75** C

transbordador espacial **75** 14

transcripción **43** 15

transformador **80** 25

transmisión automática **50** A

transmisión manual **50** B

transparencias **100** 12

transportador **49** 17

el transporte público **54**, **55**

tranvía **55** 30

tranvía aéreo **55** 31

tranvía tirado por cable **55** 32

trapos **35** 4

tráquea **5** 60

trasero **23** 19, **93** 34

traspalar **26** 13

tratamientos y remedios **41**

trecho **95** 19

tren **55** C, **55** 14

tren de aterrizaje **57** 15

tren subterráneo **54** B

triángulo **79** 6

triángulo recto **79** 22

tribuna del testigo **43** 18

tribunal **43** 16

tribunal del jurado **43** 20

tribunas **93** 10

triciclo **52** 6

trigal **81** 16

trigo **60** 22

trinche **81** 14

tripié **100** 9

tripode **100** 9

tripulación **75** 12

trombón **98** 23

trompa **66** 17a

trompa (del avión) **57** 8

trompeta **98** 25

tronco **61** 35b

tronillo **78** 7

trucha **65** 2

tuba **98** 27

tubo **13** 15, **35** 18, **91** 29

tubo de hule **78** 18

tubo de vidrio **78** 14

tuerca **37** 39

tulipán **60** 1

turbina **57** 11

ukulele **98** 3

un cuarto **79** 31

un cuarto de pollo **11** 18

un medio **79** 30

(un par de) tijeras **101** 17

(un racimo de) uvas **8** 1

un tercio **79** 32

ungüento **41** 9

uniforme **21** 45, **92** 9

el Universo **74**

untar **17** 11

uña **4** 32, **83** 29, **98** 11a

uña del dedo del pie **5** 56

uñero **98** 11a

Urano **74** 17

usos y productos **80** C

Utah **73** 44

vaca **67** 32

vaca lechera **81** 11

vagón transportador **80** 8

vaina **6** 17a

vajilla **29** 1

válvula **52** 27

vaporera **30** 3

vaquera **81** 22

vaquero **81** 21

varilla del aceite **51** 58

varillas de uranio **80** 15

vaso **13** 20, **29** 6

vegetales **6**, **7**

vegetales mixtos **18** 16

vehículo de remolque para
  acampar **53** 16

vehículos y equipo **48** A

vejiga **5** 72

vela **29** 27, **59** 9

veleta **59** 15

vellón **13** 28

vellonera **16** 12

velocímetro **50** 10

vena **5** 68

venadito **67** 27

venado **67** 26

venda elástica **40** 13a

vendas (de gaza) **39** 24

vendedor **87** 3

vendedor(a) **86** 12

ventana **27** 7

ventanilla **46** 15, **58** 21

ventila **50** 21

ventilador **50** 21

ventilador de techo **28** 1

Venus **74** 12

Verano **26**

verbos relacionados con la cocina **31**

verbos relacionados con el deporte **96**, **97**

verbos relacionados con la escuela **77**

verbos relacionados con las estaciones
  del año **26**

verbos relacionados con el restorán **17**

verbos relacionados con el trabajo del
  hogar **38**

verdulera **84** 7

Verduras **6**, **7**

verduras mixtas **18** 16

Vermont **73** 45

vestido **20** 22

vía **54** 10

vía peatonal **44** 4

viajando en balsa **89**

viaje aéreo **56**

viaje por carretera **53**

viajero abonado **55** 17

viajero **56** 3

vibora **69** 9

víbora de cascabel **65** 10

video **100** A

videocassette (cinta) **100** 3

videograbadora **100** 4

vieja **24** 14

viento **80** 4

(con) viento **25** 13

vino **16** 19

viola **98** 8

violeta **60** 16

violín **98** 7

Virginia **73** 46

visera **50** 5

visor **91** 35

volante **50** 8

vólibol **92**, **92** 22

walkman **100** 30

Washington **73** 47

West Virginia **73** 48

Wisconsin **73** 49

Wyoming **73** 50

xylófono **98** 31

Yangtzé **71** 69

yema (del dedo) **5** 52

Yenisey **71** 65

yerba(s) **6** 9

yerbas y granos **60**

Yukón **71** 56

yuntas **23** 12

zafacón **34** 13, **44** 15

zanahoria(s) **7** 32

zancudo **63** 13

zapato **21** 49

zapatos de tacón (alto) **20** 25

zarzamoras **8** 12

zona de gol **93** 23

zoológico **87** 1

zorrillo **68** 8

zorro **68** 6

zumaque venenoso **61** 44